Robert I. Guery

From One Moment To Eternity

1st Edition, February 2015

© Copyright Mobifit GmbH, Ebmatingen, Switzerland

Table of Contents

Foreword 4

Part One: Time versus Lifetime 6

1.1.	Time as a dimension	6
1.2.	A happy life	8
1.2.1.	Nutrition	9
1.2.2.	Modesty	11
1.2.3.	Human relationships	11
1.2.4.	Variety	11
1.2.5.	Awareness of natural environment	11

Part Two: Professional Lifetime 13

2.1.	Business as a continuous process	13
2.1.1.	Customer relationships – the value of continuity	13
2.1.2.	Perseverance in business	17
2.1.3.	Flexibility in business	19
2.1.4.	Shareholder value – short- and long-term business	19
2.2.	Management as a continuous process	21
2.2.1.	The life-cycle approach	21
2.2.1.1.	The life-cycle approach in human relationships	21
2.2.1.2.	The life-cycle approach in product development	23
2.2.1.3.	The life-cycle approach in services	23
2.2.1.4.	The life-cycle approach in processes	24
2.2.2.	Cooperation and conflict management	26
2.3.	Continuous learning	28
2.3.1.	A learning culture	28
2.3.2.	A learning process	30
2.3.3.	A learning leadership	31
2.3.4.	A learning infrastructure	32
2.4.	Social competence in business	33
2.4.1.	The importance of social competence in business	33
2.4.2.	Social competence related to human resources	34
2.4.3.	Social competence related to environmental issues	36
2.4.4.	Social competence related to third-world countries	37

2.4.5.	Social competence in the industrialized countries	38

Part Three: Family Lifetime — 40

3.1.	Continuity in family life	40
3.1.1.	The value of continuity	41
3.1.2.	Perseverance	41
3.1.3.	Flexibility	41
3.1.4.	Short- and long-term aspects of family life	43
3.2	Family life – a long and continuous process	44
3.2.1.	The life-cycle approach	44
3.2.2.	Conflicts in the family	44
3.3.	The learning process	45
3.4.	Social competence	46

Part Four: Social Lifetime — 47

4.1.	Continuity in social life	47
4.1.1.	The value of continuity	47
4.1.2.	Perseverance	47
4.1.3.	Flexibility	48
4.1.4.	Short- and long-term aspects of social life	48
4.2.	Social life – an extended and permanent process	49
4.2.1.	The life-cycle approach	49
4.2.2.	Conflicts within society	50
4.3.	The learning process in society	52
4.4.	Competence in social life	52

Epilogue — 54

Foreword

Change and continuity

We talk about changes, we read and learn about changes. We feel that changes make life interesting.

Even so, do we really have as many changes in our lives as the media, schools, economists, and others suggest?

The answer is that there are only a very few "real," major changes in life; most of the changes we experience are small, part of a continuous process that goes on and on.

The best analogy for this is a movie. Movies are composed of many thousands of single pictures. If they run fast enough, the human eye cannot distinguish between the individual pictures, and we see *"*continuity." The result, the continuity, is composed of many small "changes."

Another example, analogous to the development of a product, is the moment when a single drop causes the liquid in a glass to spill over. Before the last drop, there were thousands of drops that filled up the glass almost to the top. The change occurs when the liquid spills over, but it is an event that would not happen without the continuous process that precedes it.

Although everybody has a different perception of what change is, it is fair to say that real, major changes are perceived as sudden events, occurring within a very short time. Unfortunately, such sudden changes are mostly negative, like natural or manmade disasters. Earthquakes, nuclear explosions, wars, and various kinds of accident are always experienced as sudden changes in life. And yet, when a village is destroyed in an earthquake, what is destroyed in a few seconds is the work of generations, work that is the result of a continuous process over many years.

Changes thus have many dimensions. By traveling around, we can change our environment, culture, and even our language. But in all such "changes," we also experience many common factors. As a result of globalization, the environment is becoming more and more similar wherever we are. New buildings all over the world are often very similar; offices and businesses are furnished in the same way in order to make it easier for those of us undergoing the "change" in our environment to feel comfortable, which means moderating or even eliminating that "change." Very much the same applies to culture. We can watch the same performances in theaters, opera houses, cinemas, or rock venues in most western countries, and some countries are joining the western world with enthusiasm. With regard to language, English is becoming the shared language of most countries, making it possible to move without change, although other important languages, such as Chinese, Indian, French, Spanish, and German, remain.

Thus, the real issue is to distinguish between continuity and change. Is there a valid difference between the two? The notion of change is definitely a subjective one. The older we get, the more likely it is that we experience a feeling of *déjà vu,* of the fact that a change is not really a change because it is very similar to an event that has already happened before. But to put our experience into perspective, we have to remember that the average life expectancy is only 80 years, compared to the evolution of plants and animals that started about 500 Million years ago! Therefore, the true limitation to our potential, to perceiving a situation as a continuous one or as a change, is caused by our physical or psychological capabilities as human beings.

"Managing Change" and similar slogans are bound to be attractive to us. In this book, I will try to focus on a very important aspect of our life – continuity. However, the interaction that occurs between change and continuity will pervade this book from beginning to end, because there is no change without continuity and no continuity without change, just as there is no evil without good and no good without evil. By "change," we understand the beginning of a new phase, and by "continuity," we mean a return to "normality" after the change has taken place.

The true challenge in this book is to define the difference between continuity and change. As said above, the perception of this difference depends on our own characteristics, such as our age, sex, culture, and more. Consequently, I am sure that readers will have different opinions about the views expressed in this work. In spite of that, I hope and trust that persons reading this book will see life in another dimension by the time they have finished it. I also hope that by having written this book I have been able to make a small contribution toward understanding life and our environment in a different way.

Part One: Time versus Lifetime

Yesterday is History
Tomorrow is a Mystery
Today is a Gift

1.1.   <u>Time as a dimension</u>

"Everywhere is within walking distance, if you have the time."[1]
 "Life, if you know how to use it, is long."

I once heard it said in a TV discussion that only the very rich and very poor have time at their disposal. Others are driven by the economic and social systems they inhabit.

I disagree with this statement.

Time is the only real asset in life, because it is irreplaceable and the only asset that is distributed to everybody on an equal basis. True, some of us have a longer life than others do, but this is not necessarily the result of wealth or poverty. Because time is the only real asset we have, we should handle it with extreme care. The real "marketplace" for us should be "time against time" rather than "goods against money."

Time is running; every second, every minute, every hour, every day, it runs at the same pace for everybody. For rich or poor, for ill or healthy, for black or white, for young or old, physically and objectively it runs at the same speed. In absolute terms, this is the only right, and yet it does not apply to "my time." My time is limited, and so, subjectively it is running faster. My only option to "slow down" the pace is to compress "more" into a certain time unit. The continuity of time is given, but the way of changing that lies in our hands. The name of the game is to find the right number of "changes" to compress into a given time unit. This is achieved through concentration. In this way, we do not waste our time, regardless of whether we are young or old, more or less educated, female or male, or have any other distinguishing characteristics. Through concentration, we add life to our years, instead of adding years to our life by medical means.

The *daily* time at our disposal is the same for everybody.[2] However, the way we use our time varies from one person to another. Some of us are very efficient in using time, but most of us are not really aware how precious this asset is.

The best business in the world would be a business that sold real time. How many times have we heard people say, "If only I could stop time," "If only I could turn back the clock"? Unfortunately, we cannot do that. However, what we can do is use our limited time as efficiently as possible, from this moment on. The future is starting this very second!

---

[1] www.brainy**quote**.com/**quotes**/.../**steven_wright**.html
[2] www.**malik**-management.com/de/ueber-uns/.../buecher/weitere-buecher

Can you catch time?

At the same time, we need to realize that a certain process needs a certain time. If we think about the growth of plants, of children, of enterprises, we can see that they need time to reach a certain stage. The same applies to mental evolution, resulting in our educational level. We need a certain time to finish a piece of work, to find a suitable job, to reach professional competence, i.e., time plays a central role in our whole life. If we do not appreciate and accept this fact, we get into difficulties.

Often we try to accelerate a process by artificial means. The results are mostly disappointing. During the acceleration phase, side effects appear, and at the end, less is achieved than would have been possible had we let the process progress without intervention.

According to Indian meditative philosophy, every day is like a new life. Every morning is a new beginning, a new chance, like a child that opens his eyes for the first time. We reach the zenith at noontime, and in the afternoon it starts to get dark. We can consider every day as a continuity and have to take every day as a whole life. If we could not make it today, tomorrow we have another chance. A year is like 365 new lives; therefore, we always have new chances. For the same reason, however, we should not plan too far, because more often than not life is different from what we expect.

However, there are a few means that allow us to stretch time, all of them to do with feelings and memories rather than physical dimensions. First of all, feelings and memories are long living, whereas facts and figures are merely short-term phenomena. How many of us remember the name of the first IBM manager? And how many remember Mozart, Schubert, or Beethoven? Memories are the only dimensions that can override time. We bear people in mind after they have died, we feel like they are still with us, we imagine that they talk to us or are engaged in activities we remember. Dreams are also memories, connected mostly with the past, but we feel like they are happening right now.

This dimension of memories and dreams plays an extremely important role in our life. Who has no dreams? Who has no memories? These are ways to escape from the sober reality that the clock is ticking and there is no way to stop it. We give ourselves a short period of relief from the daily routine, engaging in a form of imaginary recreation that gives us the fresh energy to deal with the ongoing problems of real life. This process of alternation is a proven way of dealing with stress situations efficiently. By "diving" into a dream world, or into refreshing memories, before returning to the "real world," we can master such situations much easier than by focusing on the stressing factors themselves.

Time heals. As it advances, our physical and psychological injuries are cured and we feel better. This is a fact that we cannot change and have to be aware of. Thus, patience is an essential feature in our lives.

1.2. A happy life

Life is continuity. From the day we are born until the day we leave this world, we are going our own way. We go through our personal development, which includes education in all its forms. We build up relationships and, hopefully, give back to society at least as much as we have received from it. Although each of us possesses specific genetic characteristics (posture, look, ways of expression) that stay with us for our whole life, we can improve our quality of life considerably by an attitudinal approach, by enriching life with joy and happiness.

What makes us happy in life? Wealth, status, or success in our profession? There are countless definitions of happiness and again this is a subjective feeling that cannot be exactly defined. In my opinion, there are two main components in happiness, one physical, the other mental. Both of them are tied up closely but can be detected separately.

1.2.1. Nutrition

Many of us believe that our physical appearance is the result of genetic factors. While this is true to a certain extent, we can have considerable influence over the way we look. I want to focus on those factors that are extensively under our own control, and the most important of these is without doubt our nutrition. I have been able to experience, in the case of my own body, the difference that nutrition can make in life and how much proper nutrition can add to the quality of life.

In today's life, we have an enormous range of food to choose from. It is exactly this fact that makes it difficult to select the right components for optimal nutrition, particularly because the "right" nutrition is different for everybody. I am not going to suggest the perfect diet for you because you can find thousands of books, pamphlets, brochures, and recipes containing diets, of which not one is likely to suit you perfectly. The reason for that is that everybody has a different body; everybody has to find out for themselves what their optimal diet is.

However, I want to focus on one factor that causes the most problems with diets. This is the issue of continuity, or of permanence, which will accompany us through this whole book.

I am convinced that everybody could adopt a healthier life style and lose a few pounds by applying a certain diet. We need a "kick" in our life to start such a diet. Usually, it is an illness, a change in lifestyle, or a change in the environment that motivates us to start a diet. The beginning is hard, but most of us manage to lose most of the excessive weight, and we are happy. We are so happy that we go back to our old habits, eat excessively, and put the weight right back on. We are back to square one. So what happened here? As is well known, one of the most difficult tasks in life is to change a person's habits. Hence, although we can apply a "shock therapy" and lose weight, we return to the old situation as soon as the reason for the diet has disappeared, or at least once we think it has disappeared.

The real issue is keeping our new weight and not putting on more weight again. How can this difficult goal be reached? The only way is determination and perseverance. If we can succeed in motivating ourselves enough not to go back to the old habits, we can make it. If we can appreciate the great advantages and the increase in the quality of life we can attain by keeping our weight down, we may be able to succeed. This means going through life with open eyes and realizing every minute what is happening around us. We have to pay attention to subconscious "signals" because it is our body or soul that gives us warning signs. An illness such as cancer can be present in our body for up to eight years before it becomes clearly visible. During this time, we have countless opportunities to bring the advancing illness to a halt. We can change our habits of eating, we can stop smoking, we can participate in more sports, and we can reduce our stress; all this is in our hands. However, whatever we do, we have to do it not just for a day, or for a week or a month, but for the rest of our lives! This is what I mean by continuity in life.

The notion of "fast food" (convenience food) suggests food that is prepared under conditions of mass production and which is consumed, on the whole, in a rush. However, part of proper nutrition involves taking time for the consumption of food and to use meal times for socializing. The counterpart to fast food is "slow food," a philosophy that was established in the mid-eighties. About 60,000 followers in 42 countries participate in the movement now. They respect the seasoning, the tradition, the natural taste of food, the influence of nutrition on health, and the environmental aspects of food production and consumption, including the importance of sustainable agriculture. They prefer fruit and vegetables grown in their own country and do not consume preserved food.

The above examples apply to many principal issues in our life. Life is a mosaic, put together from many small stones, and if we want to have a meaningful and happy life, it is the whole mosaic that presents us with a complete and beautiful picture: happiness in life.

Therefore it is very important, but also difficult, to take care of every single stone during one's lifetime, in order to keep happiness as long and as profoundly as possible.

1.2.2. Modesty

In today's life, it is not so fashionable to be modest. In our western democracies, we have been taught to speak up, to insist on our rights, to demand whatever we think we should get. Giving to others is an entirely different and separate issue, as is reducing our demands.

The problem is that demanding more is not making us happier. As the Bible says, "Who is really rich? The one satisfied with his share." That is how easy it is to become rich and happy! Nonetheless, there are so few of us who understand this principle and apply it in everyday life! Again, it is western culture, which is based on materialism, that is to blame, and it is clear to me that an individual cannot change this culture. However, we have it within our power to introduce a mini-culture of modesty into our own environment, i.e., by having fewer luxuries, by not changing our car every year, by not going on shopping trips several times a week, by becoming more self-supporting, and so on. There are many possible examples of ways in which we can become more modest; each of us has the own measure of what can be done and what we are willing to do. I am sure that all of us have great potential to become more modest; if we want, we can do it! Let us start modestly and immediately!

Modesty also means taking more self-responsibility. It is not the government that should take care of us; we have to take care of ourselves. We should not blame the schools, the public services, the tax authorities, the social institutions, the health insurance companies, or others for everything that is not to our taste. All those institutions are part of our life. We helped to create them because we thought they would improve life and would make our world better. If we complain, we should imagine, just for a moment, what kind of world we would have without schools, public services, and social institutions. Who would finance this whole system if we did not pay taxes?

Very often, we need a shock, like an illness or an accident, to perceive life in an intensive way, to become conscious of how insignificant one human being is in comparison with nature. It is not necessary to be religious to realize this, but people with such strong beliefs tend, under such circumstances, to be more modest and more aware of their environment than others are.

1.2.3. Human relations

We are witnessing constant shifts in our basic way of life. If we look back, let us say fifty years, we can see that we have attained levels of unprecedented wealth in the western world since then but have also created poverty in our environment and in other parts of the world. In the west, families have become smaller, the number of marriages is diminishing, and the number of divorces is increasing. The number of kids is decreasing; the number of aged people is growing. This demographic weakness will remain with us for years to come and will affect earnings and savings. The population of active workers will have to take on an increased load. Social problems are increasing, and as a result of the increasing pace of professional life, there is less time left to most of us to invest in human relations. We try to solve them by spending money on solutions that seem reasonable to us but which do not require our personal involvement. We tend to demand that the government and social institutions solve the existing social problems.

A phenomenon that we can observe mainly among elderly people is an increase in pet ownership. While it is wonderful to have a relationship with animals, this is not a substitution for human relations. Of course, a pet is less demanding than a human being, but a "talk" to a pet cannot replace a discussion with a person who happens to be a good friend. Most of us have a small number of really good friends, usually from our school days. These friendships are long lasting because they arose independently of business or other particular interests. We simply liked some of our classmates and went through school alongside them, spending a relatively long period together. When those friends are not with us anymore, for whatever reason, we try to find other friendships, sometimes with pets.

Here, in my opinion, we miss one of the greatest chances of our time to increase our own quality of life considerably. Beside the fact that increasing loneliness creates illness, criminality, and other negative phenomena in our life, we ourselves are also a part of this process, because we, the "normal" people, become more and more isolated and have less and less contact with others. We are becoming more focused on ourselves and less interested in participating in other people's lives. What most of us do not realize is that this process makes us mentally poorer, because participating in the challenges of our fellow creatures and being able to help them are experiences that bring great satisfaction. What is more, this satisfaction makes us happy and helps us to overcome our own daily problems, caused by the facts mentioned above. Interestingly enough, giving generates greater satisfaction than taking. If you don't believe me, try it once. If you have a neighbor who is obviously suffering from an illness, or, indeed, from any other problem, try to involve him in a discussion and try to help him. If you ever have the chance, get involved in helping socially disadvantaged people in your community. You will have the greatest satisfaction you have had for a long time! And if you do this on a regular basis, you will experience a great change in your own life. You will gain self-confidence and become more joyous; people will value talking to you much more, and consequently, overall, a revaluation of your own personality will take place.

As a result of the great range of professional and economic opportunities in our western lifestyle, young people in particular are often not ready to enter a steady relationship, such as marriage, because of the fear that personal freedom will be limited by such a decision. It is precisely this attitude that time and again causes problems in marriages that end, in some cases, in divorce.

To enter and maintain a long-lasting relationship is one of the most difficult challenges in life and needs constant effort, day by day, year by year. To sustain such a relationship successfully is the most rewarding present in our life, however. Of course, at a young age, we do not realize how important such a relationship is. We have many options and opportunities, we have far more choices than in our later years. Nurturing a long-time liaison is a long-term investment, requiring great and constant effort, but with a high return on that investment.

1.2.4. Variety

A monotonous life can cause stress. We do not have a goal in sight; instead, we just go on with our daily routine and do not make any attempt to undertake something different.

It is a known and proven fact that variety in life adds to our ability to master challenges, stress, and frustration. If we engage in unusual activities several times a week, such as sports, theater-going, concerts, and social activities, we get a sense of relief that helps us to carry on with our daily routine.

The often-heard excuse for not diversifying our activities is the claim that, "I am tired in the evening, because I work too hard." This attitude is destructive and sends us into a vicious circle, because as long as we are unwilling to undertake something different, we will sink deeper and deeper into the routine that fails to provide satisfaction, and we will get more and more tired of it as a result. So, the name of the game is to break out of this circle and to change the routine. Again, the decision to do so is ours. We do not need any external help.

An important point is that deviations from a routine should not become a routine in their own right. If we go jogging every day at 19.00 pm, very soon we'll get fed up with it. If we are smart, we will not go jogging on a routine basis. We will alternate among different kinds of sports, cultural, and social activities. Even if we are not experts in every one of them, as time goes on, we will acquire a reasonable knowledge in most of them.

Variety must be a part of life, just as routine is. We have to diversify deliberately and constantly. In this way, we improve our quality of life by our own means.

1.2.5. Awareness of the natural environment

We have only one nature!

Nature on earth started to take shape about 3.5 billion years ago. The evolution of nature is an incredible miracle and reaches out far beyond human understanding. Even with the present state of gene technology and other natural sciences, we are only scratching the surface of nature. Observing nature intentionally may help us to gain security in our everyday lives, because it brings us back to our roots. Modern life is changing quite fast, but the basic components of nature are constant. The sun, the sky, plants, animals, air, and water were already here millions of years ago. Watching the environment intensively causes immediate modesty, because it helps us to understand the dimensions and colossal power of nature. It also motivates us to take care of our environment, because without nature there is no life on this planet. The better we take care of the environment, the better is our quality of life.

Mankind is only a tiny fraction of nature!

Of course, with regard to nature, there is a conflict between the economy and our individual interests. On the one hand, we would like to have a wonderful and clean environment around us, but on the other hand we have to face such challenges as the constantly growing population on earth and the negative effects of modern life, like emissions from cars, heating, and industrial plants, as well as the pollution of water and deforestation.

It is precisely this conflict that gives us the opportunity to become active and to do something for the society to which we belong. Modern media like Facebook and Twitter grant us the chance to create a group around us that shares our opinions and is ready to become active in order to correct an existing problem. Through such activity, we also reach our personal goals of human relationships and variety in our lives.

Part Two: Professional Lifetime

"A diamond is a piece of coal that stuck to the job."[3]

2.1. Business as a continuous process

2.1.1. Customer relationships – the value of continuity

A good business is built on:

- Good products
- Good customers
- Good people in the company

Good products are a prerequisite in business life, and the assumption is that all competitors are able to provide, over a long period, goods and services of reasonable quality to their customers. Otherwise, those competitors would not be able to survive. From time to time, there are disturbances in the market caused by new competitors who are not able to live up to their promises concerning quality. They can do a lot of harm to the market place in the short term, but usually they get out of business after a relatively short period.

As for good customers, we hear in every sales educational program that there are two ways to conduct a profitable and growing business:

- Finding new customers all the time or
- Keeping your old customers

It is widely acknowledged that gaining new customers is much more expensive than keeping old ones. In spite of this, many existing customers are neglected by companies and are lost as a potential source of new business. What are the main reasons for this shortcoming?

1. Frequent changes of sales personnel in the company.
2. Lack of awareness as to the importance of personal contacts with customers.
3. Difficulty in meeting all the wishes of existing customers.
4. Unpleasant experiences with existing customers.
5. Personal and intensive contact with existing customers costs money, and the result is not always visible in the short term.
6. Lack of a thorough customer analysis in the company.
7. A personal "motivation" to find new customers.
8. Financial incentives to win new customers.
9. Management requires the identification of new customers.

For the sake of fairness, it must be mentioned that there are sound reasons for recruiting new customers: changes in the nature of the business, changes in the supply range, generational changes among existing customers, and the basic management principle of creating a wide enough customer basis to make a particular business feasible.

Nevertheless, existing customers are often lost to the competition because of the above-mentioned deficiencies. Therefore, it is essential to indicate possible solutions:

---
[3] www.goodreads.com/.../282296

Frequent changes of sales personnel

People like continuity, in every place, at every time, and so we like to deal with the same person for as long as possible because we know him and all his strengths and weaknesses. Over time, we build up mutual confidence, and it is much easier to do business based on confidence.

By contrast, if we always have to deal with a new person, we have to start every time from square one and go through the same process over and over with different people. We have to build confidence repeatedly, which is not always easy and always takes time.

From a practical point of view, with frequent changes of staff, know-how is lost, because a sales person who deals with a customer for years is familiar not only with the company and its products, but also with the customer's problems, his attitudes, his needs, and his future projects. In this way, the sales person has a competitive edge over others dealing with this customer for the first time.

Lack of awareness as to the importance of personal contacts with customers

Here lies one of the major problems in today's business life. Everything changes, and changes often – even too often. Managers change, and personnel change, at every level. Because of these constant changes, we do not have time to build up personal relationships with our customers and we even do not think that it is necessary, because we have never had the opportunity to enter into such a relationship.

The truth is that even today, most of the important business is done on a person-to-person basis. The smart companies realize this and invest in their most important asset: intellectual capital. They know that without good people, there is no business, and so they keep their employees with the company by all means. Every member of the staff is kept aware every day of the importance of the customer relationship and knows that, at the end of the day, it is satisfied customers who pay their salaries and bonuses. More than that, those customers also constitute so-called "customer capital,"[4] the potential for future business. Therefore, the customer relationship has to be given the highest priority by top management.

Difficulty in meeting all the wishes of existing customers

Customers are demanding. They always have been. They have special wishes all the time. They expect that because we have built up a long-lasting relationship with them over the years, we will fulfil those wishes, and they find it difficult to understand our excuses when we can't do it.

There are two ways to deal with these wishes:

- Either we reject them and, eventually, lose a customer, or
- We regard the fulfilment of such wishes as an opportunity to have another satisfied customer who will continue to do business with us for years to come.

Obviously, the second way is the efficient and profitable one, mainly because, as mentioned above, it is much cheaper to keep an existing customer than to acquire a new

---

[4] www.montague.com/abstracts/edvin.html

one. It is also the case, however, that fulfilling those wishes will give the sales team or other staff personal satisfaction and motivation ("Yes, I can do it!").

Unpleasant experiences with existing customers

The longer we deal with a certain customer or, indeed, a person in general, the more chance we have that something will go wrong. This can happen on either side. The biggest mistake would be to bring a fruitful liaison to an end because of a single unpleasant experience. Here lies our chance to discuss this incident openly and to try to avoid similar occurrences in the future. Long-term, honest discussions are always appreciated and help to maintain a sustainable relationship with customers. The alternative would be a breakdown in communication with this customer. In this case, we have to find a new customer instead and there is absolutely no guarantee that a similar experience will not occur with the new customer.

Personal and intensive contact with existing customers costs money

Of course it costs money! But it pays off!

Personal contacts are not emails or letters. They have to be personal. We have to visit customers regularly, week after week, month after month, and year after year! If we stop, some of our smart competitors will step in, and then we'll have one customer less to visit.

"It is all about people." This saying is valid in all spheres of our life, including sales. Those who are able to establish good personal connections with customers are the winners in business. This means constant hard work and investment in resources, but the payback justifies all this. In the long term, the return on investment is very high.

The problem lies in the fact that the results of this ongoing effort are not always visible in the short term. This may be for a number of reasons: large projects often take years to reach the execution stage; in other cases, customers do not have an immediate demand for new investments in goods or services. The bottom line is that management sees only the costs. The easiest way to improve the bottom line in the short term is to save costs. This will be achieved in many cases not only by saving sales costs but also by saving the salary and bonus costs of the best people in the organization. Many of them are fired in order to employ "cheaper" staff instead. The consequences of this approach are only apparent later, and of course there will be many excuses afterward for the reduction in sales turnover, such as the recession, aggressive competition, or natural disasters. No manager will agree that this is a human resources problem caused by the loss of the stars in the company who boosted sales by taking care of personal relationships with customers for years on end.

The PC monitor at our workplace is no substitute for personal contacts. Analyses of A, B, and C customers are useful, but no analysis can replace a single visit to a customer and the ongoing customer service of experienced and qualified stars in the company. Managers have to be aware that becoming a star takes years and requires hard work!

Lack of thorough customer analysis in the company

By nature, every company is focused on the A customers. They are very few in number, but they typically generate 80% or more of the sales turnover. Relying on a few customers is risky. If anything goes wrong, the result can be disastrous for the company.

Furthermore, A customers also began small: "Even giants were small at the beginning." If we lack a proper analysis, we may overlook some rising companies with high potential.

So, if this is so obvious, why are there so few companies who carry out proper customer analyses?

It is not so difficult to assemble computer data and to show on beautiful charts the past situation in relation to active customers. The problem is that the future is not predictable and usually does not behave like the past. Therefore, the main issue with customer analyses is the interpretation and forecast. Past data is important, because it usually gives us a good picture of development over a long period: "If you don't know where you stand now, you also won't be able to reach your goal."

The longer the available period and the more balanced the development, the better our forecast will be. So again, the foundation is a continuous process of monitoring and maintaining close contact with customers. This close contact will also enable us to identify high-fliers, because the existing figures, together with the judgment of management and the situation of the particular customer, can indicate possible development clearly. It is our task to take care of this client, even before they become an A customer. The growth of the company may take years, but we have to accompany our client and help him to become an A customer. In this way, we secure the future of our own company for the long term.

Customer analysis must be carried out permanently and regularly. This is the point where most companies fail, because in today's business life, customers' data quickly becomes obsolete, and using outdated figures can result in big mistakes when forecasting.

The personal "motivation" to find new customers

There are frequent and abrupt changes in management nowadays. Without wanting to judge whether this is positive or negative, the fact is that new managers tend to bring in new staff. The new staff want to show results as soon as possible but also lack established contact with existing customers. Consequently, the new staff go out and try to find as many new customers as possible, often neglecting active, long-held clients, whose importance is not always appreciated or realized by this new personnel.

The result can be again devastating, because the A customers, who are carrying the company, are not taken care of in a proper way anymore. In the short term, management usually does not become aware of any difference, but eventually, when a competitor succeeds in taking away an A customer, there will be a considerable deficit in the operational results.

So, once again, continuity pays, and new management has to be very careful not to focus on short-term results.

Financial incentives to win new customers

Most companies try to motivate their sales staff by financial means to add new customers to the existing ones. This is logical and makes sense. If, however, sales staff receive a special reward for finding new customers, there is a danger that most of their efforts will be focused on this activity and that existing customers will be neglected. The logical measure to take to avoid this would be to allocate incentives for keeping good customers too. For several reasons, this is done only rarely. One of the reasons is the fact that resources required to keep a customer are difficult to measure. Another motive for the lack of such incentives could be the unspectacular nature of taking continuous care of an existing customer; such care should be taken anyway, on a routine basis. Once again, we are confronted with the fact, that a "change," i.e. finding a new customer, is much more "effective" in the eyes of a spectator than the "routine" activity of looking after an existing one, even if the "old" customer is much more important to the company than the new one.

The wrong approach: Price is everything!

One answer to this conundrum is to create an incentive system that takes care of both new and existing customers. Such systems exist in many places, but the main concern should be to ensure the presence of a monthly follow-up, with adjustment to new conditions if necessary. Incentive systems may become obsolete because of changing conditions in the business, and so management has to be aware that such systems have to be updated regularly.

Management requirement to identify new customers

This is a high-priority issue that has to be promoted constantly by management. Identifying new customers is essential for the future of a company because of the "life cycle" of each customer. As the resources of a business are limited, management has to be balanced in its support pro search for new customers. Sales staff should have enough resources to deal with the established customers who are essential for the ongoing success of the business. Every day, as part of modern marketing, we consumers receive hundreds of "special" sales promotion offers. These offers are mainly the result of management's desire to gain additional market share (i.e., to recruit new customers) and to increase sales volumes. Very soon, these promotions become routine, and the intelligent customer learns that he does not gain much by switching suppliers because his former, traditional supplier is also playing the same game with promotional offers. It is likely that he will realize before long that, overall, it is more hassle than it is worth to switch suppliers.

It needs to be repeated over and over that the key to the success of a corporation is capable members of staff. Good colleagues need continuous motivation to keep ahead of the competition. They will also, in the course of their work, identify new customers. Top management must constantly endeavor to find new ways to motivate people in the company. This effort must not stop, even for a short time, because negative results can appear very quickly. It is also difficult to start motivating people again after a period of neglect.

2.1.2. Perseverance in business

Persistence is crucial in business. It was always decisive and will remain essential in the years to come. Persistence in itself is indicative of continuity. In order to stay at the top, we have to give our best every day, every hour, every second.

Education or geniuses are essential for innovation and creativity, but they do not always pay for themselves. If we evaluate the success factors of many businesses, we find that they ensure a long period of austerity at the beginning of their history and succeed only by persistence. The more innovative a company is, the longer the initial period of difficulty may be before real success is achieved. There are famous stories, including those of the telephone and the personal computer, in which potential customers did not appreciate the value of these innovative ideas and believed that the new inventions had no chance of penetrating the market.

So, what makes the difference between a successful and an unsuccessful company or product? Is it the case that the best products win and others do not? The answer might be surprising: It is not the best product that wins but the people behind the product, the people who believe in it and have the vision and the persistence to go through the initial period of frustration and disappointment caused by a lack of acceptance in the market place. Of course, the main problem in this phase is that of resources. Are there sufficient resources to overcome the initial phase of losses? Once again, those people with vision, who are usually the entrepreneurs themselves, need to be so enthusiastic and convinced by their own idea that they are able to mobilize the necessary resources, frequently by taking out a mortgage on their home, taking a high interest loan from a bank, and/or using venture capital bound by strict conditions, among other daring steps. They do not care too much about the risks because they genuinely believe in the likelihood of their success. Today, about four in every ten start-ups survive this initial phase, which means that six out of ten are unsuccessful. These are usually the small enterprises that have good ideas or creative and innovative products but which lack a sense of reality, a proper understanding of how strong the established competition is on the market, and how traditional and conservative the market place is.

So let's not fool ourselves. Microsoft, Dell, Toyota, and others had to fight for years until they were able to become an established market player and are fighting every day to keep their leading market position. It is much easier to become market leader than to defend this position over the years. This fight is not spectacular by any means, but it needs stamina and lots of resources. As long as the leaders of these corporations are able to keep the fire burning and motivation in the company, they will succeed. If they stop even for a short time, they will lose their leading position.

One of the most successful managers in recent times was Jack Welch of General Electric. What was the secret of his success? No doubt it was persistence. He did not experience spectacular phases in his career; rather, he carried out a few, efficient restructuring, merging, and consolidation projects. He insisted throughout on the execution of each project, according to the plan, until the end and constantly evaluated them for their success. If a project was not being carried out according to the guidelines, he came back again and again and insisted without compromise on its proper implementation. He remained in the driver's seat for more than 20 years, and this fact in itself underlines his authority. Without his persistence, he would not have been able to be such a successful manager for such a long period.

2.1.3. Flexibility in business

Continuity in business has been advocated throughout this book. But what about changes, new challenges, new customers, new projects, and new processes in business? Should we stick to the existing format, or should we seize each and every new opportunity for change?

Business life alternates constantly between change and continuity. There is no change without continuity and no continuity without change. Once we are aware of this basic fact, we can automatically recognize the real importance or novelty of a particular change. Top companies schedule changes at predictable time intervals, and they have learned the basics of time-pacing.

Continuity provides security, self-confidence, and stability. These are exactly the characteristics that enable us to take calculated risks, to show flexibility toward our business partners. Therefore, a company that is lacking continuity will not be able to show flexibility without taking a considerable risk to the business. Retaining continuity should therefore not be wrongly interpreted as not taking risks and not being innovative.

Strangely enough, established and stable corporations do not always show flexibility toward their partners. In fact, this is probably the main reason for the limited life cycle of corporations. When they get big and important, companies become slow and inflexible, opening the door to small and flexible businesses to enter the market successfully. Thus, the main issue for top management should be to foster an innovative corporate culture, in which errors are allowed (but each error only once!) and everybody can afford to express his/her opinion without fear of retaliation, even if this opinion does not suit or please top management. The existing know-how in the brains of staff should be utilized in order to find new solutions to new challenges, thereby exhibiting flexibility toward the business environment in which the corporation is operating. Flexibility cannot be created by diktat, but only by empowering each and every capable person in the organization to use his/her specific know-how as far as possible.

Flexibility must start at the lowest level in the company. This does not mean countless formal meetings but a management that listens to workers on the shop floor and other employees, and which is not too proud or formal to talk with them directly during coffee breaks. Again, the effect of repetition is crucial. It is not enough to talk to your team members once a month or once a week. The dialog has to go on constantly. Grab every opportunity to talk to them, listen to them, and realize their good ideas. You will have astonishing success in your professional life!

2.1.4. Shareholder value – short- and long-term business

The term "shareholder value" has become a slogan in recent years. Everybody uses it, everybody has a different understanding of it, and often it is abused for the sake of other purposes.

The reason for such confusion around this expression is that there is a vast number of different businesses, operating in different cultures and environments under very different circumstances.

In the past, shareholders used to identify with "their" company, expecting a dividend and a modest yearly increase in the value of their shares. They regarded their shares mainly as a long-term investment that kept its worth over the years. The number of investors in shares was, compared to other private investors, relatively small. Most of the smaller private investors were in bonds, saving accounts, gold coins, and other conservative alternatives for the investment of capital.

Over time, liquidity has grown, and an enormous amount of capital became available on the financial markets, which started to hunt for high-yield investments in the short and middle run. One of the possible investments was shares, and insurance companies, pension schemes, and wealthy private investors entered the game. Suddenly, no identification with a company was required, only the maximization of profit, here and now. This phenomenon was familiar in the United States for many years, but in Europe it was strange for investors to begin with. Europeans were used to sustained investments, to thinking of the long term.

One of the effects of globalization is that financial markets work worldwide around the clock. This has been made possible by the information technology available to us today. Consequently, vast amounts of capital travel the world, restlessly looking for an ever higher return on investment. This process makes the financial markets volatile and causes abrupt and considerable ups and downs in those markets on a daily basis.

As far as capital or other financial instruments are concerned, it is possible to follow the process of daily, or even hourly, movements. The procedure is becoming complicated at the moment, as industrial production is getting involved. Investment goods, but also consumer goods, are unable to respond to such abrupt changes, for many reasons, such as their traditional markets, the heavy investment in industrial plants, the long lead time to change processes in the industry, and so on. Thus, when managers are confronted by insistent demands from new shareholders to supply shareholder value, increased profits year on year, regardless of market conditions and other constraints, they have only two options: to increase profits by increasing the sales volumes or the price of their products, or to save costs in the corporation by all means available.

Increasing sales volumes in the short term is difficult because the competition is under the same pressure, and every measure to increase sales levels will provoke a similar reaction from this very competition. To increase the sales price is even more difficult, again because of the competitive forces on the market. It is precisely out of fear of pressure from shareholders that the managers of publicly owned companies do not dare allocate considerable resources to long-term projects, because of the dread of decreasing profits. They "outsource" research, buying the technology from external specialists, the same way that their competitors do. So, at the end of the day, more or less all competitors are fighting with more or less the same products against each other in the marketplace. Customer service is not glamorous, so there is no real differentiation, and the fight is solely based on price.

In this situation, the obvious choice left for the managers is to reduce costs further. Again, however, all of them are doing the same, cutting expenses by any means possible, reducing staff and saving on customer service or any other item that is not immediately visible on the bottom line.

This cycle continues to repeat itself. Depending on the market conditions, the product's life cycle, and the economic environment, some managers may succeed in retaining the bottom line and from time to time even to increase profits. Over time, however, this becomes more and more difficult, because the company loses momentum as a result of having fewer and fewer resources. Inevitably, the day comes when management is replaced by a new one and the above described process starts again.

Obviously, this game cannot go on forever, and it is certain that in this sense the pressure of the shareholders on management is devastating. At the end of the day, there is no shareholder value left over.

The danger of shareholder value

The consequence of the process described above is that one has to be very careful to interpret the notion of shareholder value correctly. If shareholders are not circumspect enough, they can arrive at an unwanted situation for the corporation in which their whole investment becomes worthless. This was definitely not their goal when they started to insist on shareholder value in this very company.

The term "shareholder value" is often replaced by "stakeholder value." Although a stakeholder is not necessarily also a shareholder, this change of concepts is intended to express the belief that everyone involved, be they employees, customers, partners, investors, or society as a whole, are sitting in the same boat as the enterprise. Therefore, the main concern of shareholders should be the mid- and long-term development of the corporation and not short-term maximized profits.

Companies that are not quoted on the stock exchange have an easier life in this respect, because their shareholders are usually interested in the firm's long-term development and are less likely to put intense pressure on management to produce high profits instead of sustainable development.

2.2. Management as a continuous process

2.2.1. The life-cycle approach

The term "life cycle" itself implies continuity. We can relate the idea of a life cycle to human beings, products, services, processes, and other activities.

Successful managers adopt the principle of the life-cycle approach in all fields of management. They are focused on mid- and long-term issues and leave the daily management to their junior team members. They coach junior management but allow them enough freedom to deal with their affairs.

2.2.1.1. The life-cycle approach in human relationships

Similar to family life, it takes time and effort to build fruitful relationships based on mutual confidence between persons. It must be stressed again and again that people are the most precious asset of every business. "Nothing goes without people."[5] Given this fact, managers have to deal with their most valuable asset accordingly. First, every care has to be taken to ensure that qualified employees stay long enough in the company to contribute to the success of the business. This is easy to say but not so easy to realize. The

---

[5] www.grin.com/.../development-of-a-new-competence...

competition is also hunting for qualified specialists, promising them attractive conditions that may go well beyond present employment conditions.

So, what is the answer to this challenge? Actually it is quite complex, because the well-being of an employee depends on many factors: communication within the company and with partners outside, the work atmosphere, independence at work, interesting tasks, teamwork, an innovative attitude to challenges, financial conditions, a pleasant workplace, and many other aspects of corporate culture.

No company can be the best in all aspects of corporate culture, but by observing successful businesses, one can see that their management cultivates intensive and extensive human contact at all levels and all times. Good communication between people can compensate to a high degree for less attractive financial conditions or a less luxurious workplace. Of course, the demands and challenges on management in its commitment to extensive communication are constant, but the rewards are high. Again, successful corporations foster a corporate culture over decades, meaning that they accompany their employees during their whole life cycle in the company, from the first day to the last. As mentioned above, the human life cycle is often connected to a product or process's life cycle, so also, in some cases, does the life cycle of a work colleague or a team come to an end with the termination of a project. It is essential that during their stay in the corporation, regardless of the place or time, they are given the opportunity to live up to the corporate culture in the most positive sense.

2.2.1.2. The life-cycle approach in product development

Product development is a continuous process usually carried out behind closed doors. Successful companies never stop developing new products and further developing existing products.

Although aggressive marketing is constantly trying to get us to buy "new" products, if we look at them closely, we find that most of them are based on technologies that have been around for a long time. The "really new" ones have been in development laboratories for years and are only "new" for us, not for the specialists in this field or in the development department itself. In certain domains, such as fashion, the designers fully admit that they base their design on "old" generations of clothing. They even repeat themselves periodically, and nobody dislikes this idea.

Conservatism is one of the basic characteristics of human beings. The vast majority do not really like abrupt changes in life. This is true when it comes to products, too. Thus, if we follow the market penetration of new products, such as the telephone, the personal computer, and the television, we will see that they struggled for at least 5–10 years on the market before becoming successful. Not even key technologies are an exception: electricity became commercially successful and widely used only about 40 years after it had been introduced to the market. This situation is no different today. There are thousands of new products around, struggling and waiting for success. Only a small percentage of them succeed, not because the rest are no good but because of other factors related to their marketing. The most recent example is the Internet. It took seven years before 30% of the American population possessed an Internet connection, yet today it is impossible in the sophisticated western world to even imagine life without Internet anymore, and its success in the middle and long terms are no longer in doubt. New key technologies will definitely be the source of momentum in future economic growth.

Another aspect of longer product life cycles is the replacement cost. If a product has a long life cycle (although it may go through minor changes during this cycle), defective items can be replaced with minimum cost and effort. In Japan, this fact has been officially recognized, and the country's ministry of trade has required industrial producers to lengthen the product life cycle of their electric appliances, computer chips, and cars to slow down the production of new versions. Scientists focused on the future of research even believe that "slowness" will become more important in the years ahead.

2.2.1.3. <u>The life-cycle approach in services</u>

Services are becoming more and more important in our lives. Software in computers, repairs to sophisticated electronic and other equipment, insurance, banking, education and travel play a central role in our daily existence.

As in the case of hardware (products), here we also face fast and abrupt changes, shorter and shorter life cycles, and growing complexity.

Good service is decisive for success!

Taking PC software as a relevant example, new generations of the same software are introduced to the market in shorter and shorter cycles. Naturally, there are always improvements in a new version, but there are also bugs. The shorter the allowed development time window for a new version is, the more chance there is for bugs. Another given fact is that users need a certain time to get acquainted with a new version, so they are less efficient in their work during the transition period. The whole administration around changing over to a new version in a corporation means the allocation of considerable resources and introduction problems that influence customer relationships, human resources, and other internal features. This is the reason why many corporations stick to "old" software that, on one hand, has almost no bugs anymore and, on the other hand, is familiar to employees.

Service personnel are very much challenged by the repairing and servicing of modern consumer household appliances. New equipment is stuffed with software, and every piece of equipment has different software. In an average household, there are 10–20 different appliances, and the common user is simply overwhelmed by this diversity, so very often he/she calls a servicer just to set the software correctly. At the same time, the service personnel are overloaded by the great variety of products they have to service, and very often the result for the customer is frustration and very high service costs. However, the only other alternative the customer has is to dispose of this piece of equipment and to buy a new one in the hope that the replacement is simpler to understand and to configure. It is a known fact that new devices are often thrown out because users do not succeed in using them. Lengthening the life cycle would definitely help servicing. It would give more time to the user and to the service staff to understand the product and the software around it thoroughly. Thus, by following the principle of continuity, we could save resources and energy.

Modern financial instruments are quite complex and require a thorough understanding in order to be operated successfully. In the past, we had shares, bonds, straightforward insurance policies, and a savings account. Today, we have all of those, but also funds, derivatives, options, futures, junk bonds, combined insurance policies, and more besides. You name them. We thus arrive at the same situation as described above for appliances. The customer does not understand the product anymore and needs an adviser, who is him/herself overloaded by the great variety of products available. Consequently, the risk is high that the consumer will buy the wrong product and lose money. In some cases, the financial consultant may even be biased because of links to a certain organization that wants to sell certain products. Thus, again, by turning to traditional products, we could ease the pain of the consumer and the consultant, thereby increasing the chances of success. This is a win-win situation and would increase the confidence of consumers in these modern financial instruments.

Another fine example is that of travel. The travel industry is one of the biggest industries today, and so it has become highly sophisticated. The basic philosophy is to offer package deals, which are usually quite convenient, worked out to the last detail. The problem begins when somebody wants an individual travel arrangement. Here we come back to the dilemma of frequent changes, more short-term-oriented than in any other industry. Just think of the "last minute" offers. Again, because of the vast diversity, nobody is in control any more. It can easily happen that booking an arrangement can cost 30–40% more in one travel agent than in another. By going back to basics—airline fares, hotel prices, and other components that are valid for a long time—we would get transparency for the customer and re-establish confidence in this industry.

The number of examples in the service domain could be endless. At the end of the day, it all boils down to greater continuity to cope with human nature at all places, cultures, and levels.

2.2.1.4. The life-cycle approach in processes

We are living in a period of so-called "integrated processes." This can be best illustrated by the evolution of an industrial product, the main phases of which are as follows:

Development ➔ Production ➔ Marketing ➔ Operation and Service ➔ Disposal and Recycling

A life-cycle approach to this whole process means interdisciplinary work and intensive cooperation between teams of specialists from the first moment of product development to the end of the life cycle, meaning disposal and recycling.

Let us analyze the different phases:

Development

Successful products are developed in such a way that all the subsequent phases receive the maximum attention. Production should be as simple and rational as possible, the product should be attractive from the functional and the design point of view, its operation should be simple, and the servicing should be fair and reasonable. The product should be made of materials that are recyclable so that the environmental aspect is also considered appropriately.

Production

As seen above, development is the most important phase in the product life cycle. In spite of that, there is a lot of room to optimize the production process. Production has to consider overall feasibility, such as manufacturing, logistics (product availability, packaging, storing, and transportation), and total quality including product reliability and appearance. There is a tendency today to outsource production in part or in its entirety. Through subcontracting, production becomes less complex but control over the process is lost. A number of very successful corporations stick to the principle of "vertical integration," whereby as many parts of the finished product as possible are manufactured by the production company itself. This is not the easy way to go, but in the long run these companies retain proper control over the production process. Many of those companies that have outsourced production entirely are not around anymore. From the above it is clear that there are many challenges in the production process itself, and the greatest of these is not to consider this process as a cycle in itself.

Marketing

The later we are in a product's life cycle, the more parameters are already presented to the functional part of the organization dealing with the product. In the following considerations, the sales function is a part of marketing.

One of the main tasks of marketing is to stress the competitive edge that a particular (successful) product offers to the customer. Having said that, it is clear that successful marketing has to be honest and long-term-oriented. Because the previous phases are truly optimized, marketing can afford to act in such a manner, so a continuous and determined effort in marketing will lead to success in the sales of the product and the whole process life cycle will be increased optimally.

Operation and service

This is the process phase in which it is demonstrated that development and production made a good job and that marketing was telling the truth. Simple products are difficult to develop, but at the end of the day, only the benefit of easy operation and servicing makes the customer happy. Part of the story is a straightforward operation manual in which all the necessary steps for satisfactory functioning of the product are explained in detail and in different languages. Customer satisfaction can be further raised by a thorough explanation of the product to the buyer. Another important issue that is from time to time forgotten is the instant availability of spare parts.

Disposal and recycling

With the ever-growing world population and the increasing contamination of the environment, the issue of recycling of obsolete products is becoming crucial. One way is to lengthen the life cycle of a product; another is to manufacture a product in such a way that all, or at least most, of its components are fully recyclable, so that the disposed product does not put an additional burden on our living environment. Progressive manufacturers are taking back old products and using their components in the manufacture of new ones. New technologies also provide more and more ways to recycle products completely.

Conclusion

The above considerations show that a process cannot be looked upon any more as a sequence of single steps. Rather, the whole life cycle has to be taken into account when planning a successful process. Further, it is proven that big leaps are actually rare in business life. If we analyze so-called "quantum leaps," such as transistors, nanotechnology, DNA analysis, and so on, we find that they only emerged "suddenly" because of intensive research that had been going on day and night for years and years.

Financial "products" and other commodities in the field of services may have a "shorter" and less complicated process life cycle than industrial goods do, but the above analysis of the various phases in the process life cycle applies in principle to those "virtual" goods, too.

2.2.2. Cooperation and conflict management

As we will see below, there is no way around conflicts in a corporation. However, there is a way to keep the number of conflicts to a minimum, through the appropriate management measures.

What are the reasons for the inevitable conflicts in a business? People in the company have different interests, values, and opinions. Furthermore, they can belong to different races, cultures, age groups, and social backgrounds.

Conflict itself is not necessarily harmful. On the contrary, in a project team dealing with non-routine matters, conflicts are expected and are part of the innovation process while creating something new.

Conflicts are omnipresent in our world!

Nonetheless, no unnecessary conflicts should be created because the conflict itself absorbs a considerable amount of resources and can lead to unpleasant personal confrontations. In particular, conflicts should not be created by organizational hierarchy, i.e., by management itself. Management has to be firm and to stick to agreed values in the corporation. There is no compromise about that, even if short-term conflicts appear among staff. Only clear values can serve in the long run as guidelines, and the members of the organization have to belong to a group that is united by those values. A steady management culture gives staff a feeling of confidence and stability and helps them to master necessary changes, such as a new process or product in development. An analogy might be a "big family." A family goes through natural changes (birth, growth, education, marriage, profession, aging, death), but the continuity of the family unit is provided by the past, present, and future generations.

Management style has an immense influence on conflicts in a corporation. A good manager focuses on the strength of each of his team members. He/she builds up a long-lasting and continuous relationship with those members. In addition, care is taken that there are not "too many balls in the air," that the team focuses on one process after another. The alternative would be an authoritarian style in which the manager gives orders or manipulates and overloads his subordinates. Both will typically cause frustration and confusion and lead to sudden changes in the business, to leaps and bounds, which are, on the whole, detrimental in the long run.

Even when applying the proper management style, "continuity" may also have negative aspects, and a high-quality manager should take care that his team members are not constantly overworked and exhausted; otherwise, the best staff members on the team will be lost, sooner or later.

Different opinions on a team are normal and lead to fruitful discussions, resulting in new ideas and creative approaches. Successful companies even promote challenging discussions in which people have different opinions. The name of the game is to find out which attitude is best suited for coping with a particular challenge. The biggest mistake is not to consider somebody's opinion because it does not fit with our own. Many good ideas have gone lost in businesses because of such an attitude. It also needs mentioning that creative people by their very nature create many conflicts in an organization. They come with new ideas but are often theoretical, leaving the execution of the ideas to somebody else, who has to take care of all the details. In spite of this natural conflict between "inspiration" and "transpiration,"[6] ideas must be tested by experienced specialists who are also able to assess the resources necessary and to pursue their realization in order to be sure that no idea is lost because of a lack of ability to achieve it.

Like a variety of opinions, a variety of interests also prevail in a company. It can be assumed that the personal interests of everyone in a team are unique to that person. The key issue in a team is to find common interests and to focus on those instead of on the individual interests of the team members. Such an interest could be, for example, the creation of a truly new product that would add to the fame of all individuals in the team.

In our globalized world, more and more multiracial and multicultural teams are working on the same project. Obviously, the participants have very different intellectual and social values, and it is not always easy for every team member to understand those of everyone else. Here, again, the solution is to focus on the task and not to become personal. Tolerance is required in every area of life and by being tolerant of other races, we add quality to our own lives. The evolution of mankind is a matter of millions of years, and all the present races have existed for ages. Therefore, nobody has the right to consider another race as inferior. If a company takes care of social performance, that is, if there is no discrimination of any kind among the employees, then many potential conflicts can be avoided before they start. Unfortunately, in many places, female employees are still unequal to males, and in spite of all the efforts in this respect, the reality is not yet satisfactory.

---

[6] Edison, Thomas Alva 1847–1931

The human life cycle causes natural generational changes in the workplace. In recent years, accelerated by information technology, the generational changes have taken place much faster than they did before. In addition, an attitude of derogation toward the "old" people could be sensed in many places. Older people were fired during periods of recession, only for firms to find out later that an enormous volume of know-how had been eliminated by this process, with serious consequences in many corporations. There is a return to normal age distributions in businesses again, but the damage has been done and it will take years before we reach the former situation. Young managers have to take care that this harmful process does not repeat itself in the future and that the older and younger generations really cooperate in the workplace, taking advantage of the creativity and energy of the young people as well as the know-how and experience of the older generation. This process can be even witnessed in the evolution of the "e-economy." It has been proven that the "new" economy cannot be detached from the old one. The transition has to take place gradually in order to avoid difficulties and even the collapse of certain branches.

2.3. Continuous learning

Do we earn to learn or learn to earn?

There is no definite answer to this question, but I shall try below to provide at least partial answers.

Many generations have been accustomed to the conventional form of education:

(Kindergarten) ➜ *(Primary school)* ➜ *(Secondary school)* ➜ *(High school)* ➜ *(University)*

The amount of information and knowledge received at the different levels used to be sufficient for the whole professional life cycle of a particular individual.

The last two generations have increasingly had to face the problem that the life cycle of knowledge is becoming shorter and shorter and the usual mode of learning is not adequate any more. This process is accelerating, and today it is clear to every university graduate that even immediately after receiving their university degree, the learning must continue. Learning has to accompany professionals at almost every level throughout their entire professional life. Continuous learning has become a part of our life and the center of gravity has shifted from the traditional institutions of education to specialists in certain fields and to the companies employing specialists of all kinds.

2.3.1. A learning culture

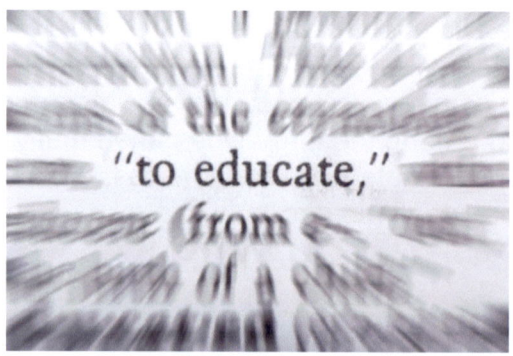

Learning never stops!

A learning culture emerges from processes and organizational systems. Both are dynamic and subject to constant changes. Therefore, it is particularly important to monitor processes and to receive feedback about the success and the results of learning programs.

A learning culture is often created by curiosity. Thanks to an individual or a group of curious people eager to acquire new knowledge, such a culture can spread through a corporation, a family, or any other organization. Modern learning is integrated into our lives and careers. Coaching is provided as a rule, and there is interaction between technology and human beings, and between ethnic and age groups.

This culture can also be extended by people who want to improve their own level of knowledge and thereby become better in their professional field. They are aware of the fact that continuous learning increases their market value, prolongs their (otherwise limited) professional life cycle, adds significantly to their job satisfaction, and creates a greater freedom to choose suitable jobs. Additional knowledge adds to the flexibility of an individual, is self-motivating, and creates personal satisfaction. It is the only asset that no crash on the stock exchange market or any other external disaster can eliminate. Continuous learning has a great influence on one's lifestyle. Just think of reading, attending professional courses, or interactive learning on the computer as an alternative to watching a football match on the TV, spending hours in a bar or disco, or playing games on the computer. Without judging what is better, there is no doubt that the mentioned lifestyles are very much different.

A learning culture also includes "soft knowledge." This is something out there that we are either born with (in relatively few cases) or which we learn through many years' experience. This is the art of dealing with people. This is not fact-based knowledge but much more intuitive and commonsensical but which nevertheless has to be applied in a focused and continual way. The importance of this quality cannot be stressed enough. It helps us in our private and professional lives to succeed and to achieve more, but also to get more personal satisfaction in all aspects of our lives.

Continuous (lifelong) learning also means learning after retirement, indeed, until the last day of our lives. The value of a learning culture during the professional life cycle is extended to an additional, increasingly important phase of life, which is getting longer and longer for an aging population. Not only will retired persons no longer have the feeling that they are superfluous, but by acquiring new knowledge they can start new activities, or even a new career, that may give them newfound satisfaction. A learning culture will give these people fulfilment and happiness in their lives, instead of frustration and disappointment. They will be able to persist and keep in contact with other persons or groups who may have the same interests in learning or applying the newly acquired knowledge.

A learning culture even has a purely materialistic aspect. Rich people nowadays are mainly those who possess a great deal of knowledge and information. By virtue of the natural limitations on the number of people who are prepared to devote a considerable share of their life to learning, we can see the establishment of a professional elite that, while limited in their professional life cycle, achieve extraordinarily high earnings during that limited period. Of course, they understand perfectly the need to use that acquired knowledge only as a basis and to create new knowledge and innovative processes that go beyond common knowledge.

2.3.2. A learning process

The correct learning process includes the following phases:

Acquiring ➔ *Sharing* ➔ *Applying (Using) knowledge.*

It is generally understood that the learning process is similar to a chain reaction. The more we know, the more knowledge we can generate. In order to acquire as much knowledge as possible in the shortest possible time, we create learning teams and use data- and knowledge bases, such as the Internet. Teams generate continuity in learning and, by completely integrating each member, the total amount of knowledge in the team is much higher than the sum of the individual contributions. Naturally, such a process is a competitive one, and team members are exposed to rivalry, with some risks for the weaker personalities in the team.

Top professionals, whether in art, management, or politics, are individuals who follow a learning process their whole career, sometimes even their whole life, with immense determination. They typically have a strong sense of discipline and stick to their targets day by day, week by week, year by year. They are not necessarily more talented than other professionals, but they grow to be the best because of their devotion, persistence, and discipline, which are high among their priorities. They often sacrifice pleasure or enjoyment in their lives for their commitment. This is becoming the rule in many cases because, in real life, there is less and less time left for learning. Nowadays, this lack of time can become critical for individuals, especially in the technology field, because the life cycle of knowledge is shortened every year, and even a university education becomes obsolete within a short period. We simply do not have the time to learn everything. We are forced to learn in a goal-oriented fashion and quickly. This is "just in time" learning.

Interactive learning on the Internet or in other institutions creates learning communities and platforms. An enormous amount of knowledge that has been gathered by many capable persons over a long period is available to practically everybody. Discussion forums allow for the real-time sharing of knowledge. Question and Answer (Q&A) features on the web enable us to partake of the know-how of other people dealing with similar or identical problems and to avoid in this way failures that would occur because of our lack of relevant experience. Of course, this does not mean that we do not make mistakes any more. On the contrary, we should be allowed to fail from time to time, in order to learn from our failures. In this way, we can generate additional skills for ourselves, while also dealing with very small details that might be crucial to a specific process and which cannot be acquired from other sources. This specific know-how can be shared with other people inside and outside the organization and help in proper implementation of projects.

Modern schools engage an increasing number of professional researchers in specific subjects that their scholars are interested in. This technique allows for more efficient and goal-oriented instant learning. In this way, students are prepared more efficiently for their professional career.

Institutions, enterprises, and other organizations usually have large and important databases at their disposal. Because of the increased pace of business, political, and social life, constant and competent updating of those databases plays a central role in the efficiency of the organization. Unfortunately, this duty is not always and everywhere recognized and is often neglected. The negative results of this negligence can be seen in the organization's subsequent lack of success.

E-Learning is gaining momentum because it can be suited to the specific needs of the corporation. To make it a reality and user friendly means a considerable investment in resources, so smaller companies will still use conventional means of learning, such as school classes, seminars, books, etc.

Today's e-Learning comprises four main streams:
1. Computer-Based Training (CBT).[7] This provides external multimedia learning software solutions.
2. Web-Based Training (WBT). This provides multimedia learning software solutions on the Internet or Intranet.
3. Virtual Classroom. Audio and Video Conferences, Business TV, Newsgroups.
4. Learning Management Systems (LMS). Databases containing learning software solutions combined with search criteria and download features.

E-Learning offers new opportunities to corporations but also comes with some risks. Students can set their own time and choose their own learning and working hours. Further e-Learning occurs independently of place and provides opportunities for communication with tutors at any time. A good tutorial guide helps the student to set priorities and to find the most efficient way to tackle a new task. E-Learning can be risky if support from tutors is not adequate. A lack of tutorials can also cause problems. Searching can take a lot of time if search engines are not adapted to this purpose.

Traditional means of learning do not lose market share to e-Learning. Rather, schools are striving for integrated systems, whereby a combination of the two components is created. For instance, a school can equalize the starting level of participants in learning programs by distributing material, case studies, etc., over the Internet before the beginning of a seminar. The seminar itself is conducted mainly by conventional means of learning. After finishing the seminar, participants keep in touch over the Internet, evaluate team solutions to a case, and discuss the solution or its implementation.

Polls show that alongside the growing popularity of e-Learning in business, the resources spent on traditional learning methods are increasing.[7] The "learning society" is no longer just a slogan. If anybody asks the question, "What happens if, after investing so much in the professional education of an employee, he leaves the company?" the proper answer is "What happens if there is no investment in education and the employee stays with the company?"

2.3.3. A learning leadership

Learning is managing. The same rules of general management also apply to learning. Learning must be fostered and must be done continuously. The task of top management is to orchestrate the learning process, and the task of middle management is to fit those processes to the short-term needs of the organization and to be open to possible new solutions.

In successful organizations, continuous learning is a part of strategic thinking. In such entities, learning is led by the heads of the organization, i.e., by the CEO or the head manager. The CEO knows that by keeping the well-educated and capable people in the company, the knowledge is also being kept there, a decisive factor in today's business life.

---

[7] de.wikipedia.org/wiki/E-Learning

The CEO also has to be careful as to the composition of the company's own learning programs. A learning program within the corporation must be competitive with those of schools, universities, and other educational institutions. It also has to be competitive with to the programs of other corporations. As an example, only part of the learning needs can be shifted onto business schools, because many of them develop the same models at the same time, so employees of different companies may be doing the same things after completing business courses. This, of course, has little to do with competition.

The responsibility of the CEO[8] is to

- Challenge senior executives to develop a learning environment and processes;
- Create learning communities;
- Promote a browsing mindset;
- Support learning commitment;
- Achieve learning leadership;
- Set innovation as a business strategy; and
- Measure the impact of learning on the bottom line.

Leadership must be exemplary!

It is not enough for top management to set the guidelines, however. There must be an efficient line of communication to line managers, who have to take care personally of the implementation of learning initiatives and programs. These same line managers also have to create a learning environment in their domains and to control the success of the learning programs.[8] They have to communicate the urgency of learning to their colleagues, and it is part of their responsibility to cascade learning in their own environment. They also have to celebrate the successes of learning programs together with the relevant staff. They have to provide remuneration for the knowledge sharing within their domain.

2.3.4. A learning infrastructure

As learning is becoming a part of corporate life, it is necessary to create an adequate learning infrastructure within enterprises. A proper infrastructure could have considerable influence on the success of learning programs or processes in companies.[8] Actually, at the very least, the firm should provide the same facilities as a school provides, but learning in

---

[8] www.imd.org/.../discoveryevents/Discovery-Event-...

teams, goal-oriented learning, and learning opportunities in general should, in the interests of the business, surpass the possibilities provided by schools.

A company's learning infrastructure must be built up in a professional way and not created accidentally. The initiative should be taken by the company and should include:

- Formal learning opportunities for employees. Such opportunities have to be pinpointed systematically and continuously and to be offered to capable members of the organization.

- Certification. Staff members who have completed a learning program must receive a certificate and be acknowledged as specialists in the specific fields included in the program.

- Coaching must be provided. Persons within the organization who possess specialist know-how should help junior members or staff joining a new team to acquire knowledge in their specific domain quickly and efficiently. It is particularly important to learn how to learn.

- Learning programs and processes have to be monitored constantly. The learning team has to be part of this evaluation in order to provide the most effective way of learning, based on constant dialog.

- Young talent employed by the company has to be given the chance to meet one another throughout the organization and to suggest solutions to problems identified within the corporation.

As to the physical facilities, they should be available and at the disposal of learning staff during, but also outside, working hours. They should comprise:

- Chat rooms with inducements to visit.

- Beer and sandwich meetings.

- Learning rooms equipped with the necessary utensils. Learning should happen in teams and not in classes.

- Facilities for the exchange of knowledge.

- Technology infrastructure, such as Internet access, broadband cables with sufficient capacity, and external access.

Successful learning in the corporation is essential for the overall success of the enterprise itself. Therefore, it cannot be stressed enough that the learning infrastructure in the company must be given very high priority by top management.

2.4. <u>Social competence in business</u>

2.4.1. <u>The importance of social competence in business</u>

Recent events in our environment indicate very clearly that in spite of the growing influence of economic forces on our life, the social element cannot be neglected. In fact, in emergency situations, the social component becomes once again the most important one, directly affecting our very existence.

Everybody understands now that it would be an illusion to separate business and society; our future depends very much on the capacity to reach an optimal synchronization between the two. Enterprises that recognized this necessity ahead of others and which are working continuously to improve their social competence in business have a competitive edge over those who only talk about such a competence or who do not even care about it.

In most cases, it is small and very small businesses that have a higher social competence, because they depend on "small" customers. However, it may be the case that in some business fields, social competence plays a less important role. Nevertheless, all businesses have to be aware that this component of business life cannot be neglected.

The importance of social competence in business has been recognized by international organizations like the United Nations and governments, but also by the economic establishment. As an example, the Dow Jones Sustainability Group Index has been created, and enterprises are rated according the criteria of this index. Enterprises that assume social responsibility and take care of the environment are often the only ones who are allowed to participate in tenders for government programs.

2.4.2. Social competence related to human resources in the enterprise

As indicated before, the most important asset of a business is its human resources. Other assets, such as buildings, production machines, computer systems, etc., can be acquired for the short term and look very much the same in different companies. By contrast, building up an efficient, motivated, and highly qualified staff is a long-term process and is decisive with regard to the competitive positioning of an enterprise on the market. Therefore, this is an important strategic issue that has to be given the highest priority by top management.

Unfortunately, the real situation is often different, and the issue of human resources is frequently neglected. The results can be disastrous, proof of which is the number of companies that have had to close down because of past failures in human resources policy.

A successful human resources policy, combined with social responsibility, has many facets. It starts with the employment of a new colleague and ends with the decease of a retired staff member. It includes the following main topics:

- Pay differentials among employees across race and gender profiles cannot exist. The only reason for such differentials is the task to be carried out and the qualifications of the person in question.

- New employees have to be brought on board with the appropriate attention and friendliness. First, the company and the workplace have to be presented and explained. Then, the new staff member has to be introduced to their colleagues and be given a coach. Then follows the introduction to the teams with which they will be cooperating.

- A pleasant work environment is part of any employee's motivation. An ergonomically correct workplace, with the possibility of adding personal touches, has to be provided. Health and safety expenditure must also be part of the policy.

- The coach has to take care that the new employee receives an adequate education in order to be able to fulfil the allocated tasks. Reference is made here to the items mentioned under "continuous learning."

- New staff members have to become part of the organization's internal communication system right from the beginning. They should be allowed and even encouraged to give feedback, suggestions, and proposals. This feedback has to be taken seriously and responded to within a short time. Performance appraisals should help employees to develop their strengths.

- The above issues have to be taken care of continuously during the employment of each and every teammate. One of the common mistakes in management is to neglect "old" employees, the valuable members of staff who contribute most to the success of the enterprise, while focusing attention on new staff.

- A corporate culture focused on human resources should include informal meetings at all levels and between the levels. Top management should be aware that management by "talking" and "walking" is not a waste of time but one of the most important sources of information about what is happening on the shop floor. Such information is essential for the avoidance and quick correction of mistakes.

Employees leave a business for various reasons. The most common is to change to another corporation. Another reason may be illness and yet another may be retirement.

- Losing a qualified and efficient employee is a real loss to the enterprise. Therefore, there must be an attempt made to keep the employee in the company. This can be done by job rotation, job enrichment, or a change in remuneration. If all those possibilities do not change the mind of the collaborator, he/she should be given all the appropriate assistance and be able to leave with honor. It is often the case that former employees will come back to a firm if they had a good experience there.

- Good companies have adequate insurance so that if somebody leaves because of an illness or an accident, the company can help him/her financially. This is an obligation that belongs in the portfolio of corporations with social responsibility.

- Last but not least, when staff members reach retirement age, they have typically been with the company for many years. They have given their best, and it should be only natural that they are able to benefit from a proper pension scheme. Such a pension scheme will have given them a feeling of security during their period of employment and will have been one of the reasons why they stayed so long with the enterprise as a motivated staff member.

It is mainly large corporations that devote resources to the active recruitment of future employees. Usually, they have continuous contact with universities or other schools and invite students from time to time to visit their facilities or to spend some time as trainees with the company. Others go even further, setting up kindergartens or schools for the children of employees. In such a way, these children grow up "with the company" and might be a natural source of highly motivated employees in the future.

2.4.3. Social competence related to environmental issues

The responsibility to take good care of our natural resources on this planet so that future generations can also use them is often covered by the notion of *sustainability*. In the following deliberations, sustainability will be illustrated by processes within in an industrial enterprise.

Because we are in some places at a critical or even irreversible point in the misuse of resources, legislation has been introduced in recent years to correct this situation or to prevent further deterioration. Unfortunately, this does not happen in all countries, and rogue organizations exploit this fact unscrupulously.

Enterprises with social responsibility had already started to target environmental issues years ago, and sometimes they are even ahead of legislation. However, coping with environmental regulation means additional costs to a corporation and it is therefore a careful balancing act to find the equilibrium between economy and ecology.

Social conscientiousness also means in this case that apart from a general responsibility, the corporation itself, as a part of society, would suffer in the long term from any short-sighted policy of overexploiting natural resources. Eventually, raw materials will become much more expensive, production sites may have to close down because of pollution, or qualified people may not wish to join the company anymore because of its bad reputation with regard to the environment.

Environmental issues thus have a direct impact on the bottom line of a corporation and touch on all the main functions of an enterprise directly, including:

- Research and Development
- Human Resources
- Production
- Logistics/Purchasing
- Marketing
- Services
- Finance

About 80% of a product is already defined at the research and development (R&D) phase. Therefore, it is extremely important that R&D staff select processes and materials that are environmentally friendly. This means materials that are readily available and do not require a lot of energy and resources to produce, processes that do not overload the environment (emissions, pollution, etc.), and products that can be fully recycled after reaching the end of their life cycle. At the same time, economic aspects must not be forgotten, and a proper balance between both demands has to be found.

Careful selection of personnel with adequate education and qualifications will assure that oversight pertaining to environmental issues and their proper integration into all activities of the enterprise will prevail. This is just one example of how important human resources are in an enterprise.

Production has a significant influence on processes. Although the basic practice is given by the product specifications, production has considerable elbow-room with regard to practical details. It is commonly the case that, during production, procedures are improved and production specialists but also shop-floor workers have a great influence on efficiency, i.e., less scrap, increased cleanliness, and suggestions for new, environmentally friendlier materials to use in the process. The more knowledgeable the production staff is in this respect, the more they are aware of environmental issues.

Transport and packing are in principle a burden for the environment. Therefore, a constant effort has to be made to minimize them. Good planning can avoid empty trucks driving around on clogged roads; transportation can often be carried out by rail, even if it means a little more shipping time. Recyclable materials for packing reduce the strain on our environment, and the overall feasibility is a given, even if sometimes the packing material itself costs a little bit more.

Environmentally friendly products can give an enterprise a competitive edge, and proper marketing should use this argument extensively. If the marketing staff are aware of this advantage and do not only focus on price, they will actually push R&D and production to create products that are more environmentally friendly, maintaining a competitive edge over time.

Service personnel are also able to contribute to the environmentally friendly behavior of an enterprise. Here again, cleanliness, suggestions for product improvement, and use of other materials can help to cope better with environmental issues. Furthermore, better instruction of staff will result in more awareness and added value for the company.

Last but not least, financial staff should be interested in the overall performance of the enterprise, including its environmental competence. Controllers have to see the whole picture and not focus on saving costs by all means. Recent developments in many industrial companies have shown how dangerous it can be in the long run to neglect environmental issues, especially in order to save costs. Physical damage and harm done to the corporate image can be immense and could even ruin a corporation. By contrast, top companies that are also leaders in environmental competence usually have a healthy bottom line.

2.4.4. Social competence related to third-world countries

The issue of the relationship between western industrial and third-world countries is a complex one that has been around for several generations now. In former days, numerous third-world countries were exploited by colonialist movements and governments. In order to prevent such an evil, the United Nations proposed in 1999 the Global Compact platform, dealing with human rights, labor, and environment.[9]

Even today there is a clear trend, mainly for cost reasons, to shift production and services to third-world countries. However, in our globalized world, it is no longer possible to detach those countries from the so-called "developed" world. What is more, a long-lasting partnership with third-world countries must be built up. Enterprises that understood this right from the beginning were able to create a win-win situation, whereby they invested considerably in resources and were thereby able to benefit from them. The process is often long and laborious, but at the end of the day it is rewarding.

Mainly large corporations active in third-world countries for many years have evaluated thorough and successful schemes to create long-lasting and fruitful relationships with employees and with the official organs and institutions of the countries in question. As

---
[9] http://www.unglobalcompact.org/

soon as production facilities employ female workers in large numbers, day nurseries and sometimes even primary schools are established in the company. In this way, mothers are relieved of their everyday problems, and children grow up within the company; they become exposed to the corporate culture at an early age. Those children often become loyal and well-educated employees, able to accomplish their tasks in a competent way.

Furthermore, local and foreign students are taken into the company temporarily and acquire knowledge and special skills during this period, becoming attractive to employers after completion of their studies. If they do not join the company where they trained, they may, on the basis of their pleasant experience, later become loyal customers, distributors, or other business friends.

Corporations often foster close relationships with universities and other schools, by coaching students and acting as mentors. In this manner, the contact between young and old takes place in a natural way. Young people can benefit from the know-how of experienced specialists in their particular field.

Outstanding employees are sent on postgraduate and other special courses in the country or abroad so that continuous learning is assured.

Professional associations are promoted and company clubs are often created for employees.

Globalization itself is a positive phenomenon, but in third-world countries in particular it can cause grave problems for society. The transition for individuals within a limited time window is much more difficult there than it is for somebody in an industrial country, who has been exposed for a long time to a higher rate of change.

2.4.5. Social competence in the industrialized countries

Industrial and highly developed countries "contribute" a great deal to the world's environmental problems, but they are also increasingly faced with social problems, caused by mergers, the reengineering of industries, and, last but not least, by the globalization process.

The phenomenon of the "working poor" in western countries is gaining importance, and governments are increasingly confronted with the challenge of dealing with the new problem of poverty in the western world. Of course, the state cannot cope with this phenomenon alone, and business organizations have to participate in finding the solutions in order to secure freedom and security in a suitable social environment, so that a stable basis for business is provided for the future.

The pace of change in business life is too fast even for well-educated and qualified individuals. We are given personal freedom, but we cannot achieve it because of the frequent and huge changes to which we are exposed. Those changes cause uncertainty and insecurity. We are no longer certain that the savings we have accumulated over many years are secure; we are not sure we really understand what is happening around us; we are not convinced that the way we act is the right way. Above all, we do not know what is going to happen even in the immediate future.

In this state of uncertainty, we are inclined to call on the state to solve our problems, forgetting, that a) the state cannot do miracles and b) the state itself is actually part of our own environment. Under these circumstances, business organizations carry a great deal of responsibility and are challenged with finding solutions (in part alongside political institutions) to social and environmental problems. Real solutions must be based on scenarios in which government and business but also other relevant individuals participate equally and actively contribute to the process itself. An interesting example of political initiatives is Israel's "Ministry for Coming Generations," which deals with issues related to the environment, sustainability, and genetics.

Again, if we take the industrial enterprise as an example, it would have following options:

Social issues

- Create a pleasant working environment.
- Make staff members part of the corporate "family."
- Communicate medium- and long-term business policy constantly and clearly.
- Promote informal communication across all levels.
- Create a transparent and fair remuneration system.
- Create reasonable pension schemes.

Environmental issues

- Establish environmental management systems with accordance with ISO 14001.
- Use the life-cycle assessment method when judging ecological measures.
- Avoid environmental pollution even if it costs money.
- Take care of groundwater sources.
- Create green space.
- Plan buildings that are environmentally friendly (i.e., energy efficient).
- Plan processes that are environmentally friendly (i.e. energy efficient).
- Reduce traffic to the minimum necessary; use public transport.

An example of a Swiss project that integrates the above-mentioned aspects is that covered in Transdisciplinary Case Study 2013[4] of the "Siemensareal" in the city of Zug (close to the railway station). For this area, the case study looked into the following aspects:

- Energy efficiency of buildings and infrastructure on the area,
- Potential needs of future residents of the area,
- Context of the area (city of Zug, region, Canton of Zug) and policy processes.

---

[10] http://www.uns.ethz.ch/translab/cs_former

Part Three: Family Lifetime

Sweet, sweet home!

3.1. Continuity in family life

Families emerge from individuals. The behavior of a family is thus the sum of the personal behaviors. Continuity in families is provided partly by inheritance. Modern research indicates that about 40–50% of the personality and behavior of an individual is determined by the genetic fingerprint of the parents. At the same time, this very same statement leads to the conclusion that the remainder is determined by the environment, of which the family is a very important part. This explains the reality experienced by practically all parents that their children, even if they look physically very similar, even twins, differ considerably in terms of their personality. The responsibility of parents toward their children is heavy, and the family is the safe haven that children rely on so much in daily life.

Business life is actually based on the family idea. We always find a close relationship between what is going on in families and in corporations. Both conform to Darwin's theory that both intense competition and immense diversity prevail in life.

Family life has changed dramatically in recent years. The large families we used to have in western countries gradually dissolved, and this phenomenon is apparent today even in third-world countries. Small families with fewer children than before, sometimes none, fewer married couples, more divorces, generally less commitment to family life, a turn away from the religion: these are the trends to which we are exposed, especially in the western hemisphere. The increasing self-centeredness of individuals is revealing serious cracks in our social structures, and the family, as part of society, is fighting against unwanted effects that result from fast and considerable changes in our environment.

3.1.1. The value of continuity in family life

In our constantly and rapidly changing world, the temptation is huge to effect changes in the family, too. Changing partners and ending relationships have become much easier than in the past.

So, why should we keep continuity at any cost in our family?

The answer is complex but can be reduced to emotional and rational aspects. With regard to the emotional aspect, there is no substitute for love and devotion in life. Giving up a relationship without really being aware of the significance of it to ourselves can result in mental anguish, with all the attendant consequences. Furthermore, we do not know whether we will be able to establish such a flourishing relationship again. As to the rational aspect, it is for sure very troublesome and costly to end an association. There is always a loss-loss situation created.

The conclusion is, then, that it is worthwhile to fight to maintain a relationship that was successful for a long time. Casual disagreements or clashes, which are often identified as triggers of a divorce or the end of a liaison, should and can be overcome in other ways. It is actually up to us whether we let a minor conflict grow into a major one until there is no way back anymore.

3.1.2. Perseverance in family life

Tradition is the family's most important asset. Children observe the behavior of their parents very carefully. It is amazing how much the way of life of children is similar to that of the parents. Parents often have the feeling that children do not want to accept their ideas and opinions, and that they are opposed to anything that comes from the parents. If they look objectively at the lifestyles of their children, however, parents can usually identify important elements of their own lifestyle. Therefore, the importance of giving an ongoing good example to their children each day cannot be stressed enough. This is by far the most effective tool for shaping the personality and behavior of our children!

Persistence means also tireless communication in the family. All important actions we take inside (and outside) the family have to be communicated to our family members. This communication has to be a part of family life and should not stop. Unpopular decisions can be made acceptable to the family if they are communicated in the proper way and the reason for the decision is explained in detail to everybody.

Continuity brings tranquility to life, but it may not become compulsory. Everyone should know his/her limits. For example, if children are preparing for a test, their parents have to prevent them from spending too long on revision because often bodies and minds cannot take too much work. The meaning of continuity is to stick to certain principles and values in life, and permanence is the alternative to rapid and frequent changes that would rob the self-confidence of a person who might think that his/her character is not steady enough to bring stability into his/her own life. The cognitive capacity of human beings is not infinite, so the tolerance for change is limited. Successful individuals focus on one process after another. Parents have to communicate these ideas to their children in order to show them the way toward a balanced life and to avoid distress as much as possible.

Biorhythms should be integrated into planning activities of children. It is possible to work out which hours are the most productive, and parents can plan the schedule of their children accordingly. They usually know whether a child is more active in the morning or in the evening and so this child's activities can be planned correspondingly.

3.1.3. Flexibility in family life

The very fact that children are so different poses a major challenge to parents. Assuming that a typical family has two children, there is a large difference between the behavior of the first and the second child. This dissimilarity grows further when a family harbors three or more children. In any case, each child needs its own private sphere, and parents, like sisters and brothers, have to honor that.

The first child is usually a "trial" child. Parents do not have any previous experience with children, so they go through a process of trial and error. Moreover, they usually push the first-born to achieve because they do not have experience with the limits and boundaries of children, and because the first-born child cannot benefit from the experiences of sisters and brothers, he/she has to fight alone for every achievement. Consequently, the first-born are usually fighters and achievers.

Second-born children are the "asking" ones. They can consult the older brother or sister if they want to know something. They are usually much softer than the first-born. In a family with three children, they are "middles," squeezed in between the oldest and youngest. In such cases, they very often have to mediate between the others, so they tend to strive for compromises; they are sociable but strong minded and sometimes feel uncomfortable about being squeezed in between two other siblings.

The third or youngest child is usually the outgoing one, the one that likes to take chances. This child is often told, "You are too young to do that" when their older siblings engage in an activity, so to prove that this is not the case, they dare to do things that other children would not. They are not the type who would look back upon their life and say, "It was boring, but I made it."

Parents have to be aware that there is a certain "order" between children. This is similar to a hierarchy in a corporation. Each child has a certain status and deals with certain tasks. This can remain in place for their whole lives, especially if they become adults without families of their own.

Another huge challenge for parents can be childhood "abnormality." This can be an inherited illness but also a behavioral problem. In these cases, parents are obliged to help their children as long as they ask for help and need it. Most important of all, parents have to treat the situation as "normal" and treat their children as the equal of others.

The micro-environment outside the family has a particular influence on children. Parents must therefore be flexible enough to accept the behavior of their children when it might be not in line with their own perceptions and values. More than that, they have to support their children generously, even in cases where they would act differently. This is the basis for a good and fruitful relationship between parents and children throughout their time together.

As to flexibility between spouses, fully equal rights for both partners must be standard. Matters concerning the family and the outside environment have to be discussed in an open and constructive manner, and in disputes, couples should try to achieve viable compromises. Working women have more fulfilment in life than do those who are full-time housewives. Sharing tasks in the family should allow wives to earn a decent living in a satisfying job.

Unusual environments, such as a shared trip abroad, allow for unusual discussions between spouses. In this way, unusual and fruitful solutions for family problems can also be found. Frequent travel adds to flexibility. By seeing new places and new cultures, we get inspirations to deal with challenges in different ways.

3.1.4. Short- and long-term aspects of family life

Aging is a continuous process. We live our lives day by day, when suddenly, one morning, we look in the mirror and have the feeling that we appear to be old. This is the reciprocity between continuity and change.

The elderly see the same changes coming back generation after generation. Parents observe time and again that children are making the same mistakes that they did, years earlier. Of course, it is often the case that children do not want to receive advice from the "older" ones, which is why they make the same mistakes.

Thinking of the life cycle of a family and of lasting partnerships within the entity called the family, it is obvious that we are dealing within this frame mainly with regard to long-lasting issues. However, as in a corporation, daily business is ongoing and ought not to be neglected. The development of a partnership between spouses, the shaping of the personality of children, the production of their education, the creation of a solid financial basis for the family, and other principal issues are all continuous processes that take a long time but are made up of many small, intricate pieces, like a complex mosaic.

Find the right balance!

In the long run, the success of the family is of such importance that it should become the highest priority in family life. The reward for grandparents, parents, and children is so huge that everything has to be done to ensure success. Having this vision shared and communicated to all family members makes it much easier to deal with everyday hassles, even if some events seem highly unpleasant when they happen. If everybody in the family understands that a special effort very often has to be undertaken to achieve this long-term goal, the motivation to undertake such an effort automatically becomes quite high.

Family life is a multifaceted matter. If we take into account all the different activities of every family member, we arrive at a highly complex network that needs ongoing cooperation and coordination at a high degree in order to achieve the set goals. Work at all levels (the external work of the family head, housework, and schoolwork and other childhood activities) is a part of family life, but leisure time (entertainment, excursions, culture) is an equally important component. We cannot imagine the existence of a successful family without taking care simultaneously and continuously of all the important issues. Consequently, "managing" a family can become quite a complicated matter. However, the biggest advantage that the family has over an enterprise is that family members usually (and hopefully) do not have commercial interests that affect their relatives. If families come into conflict over material issues, very serious difficulties can arise, even total destruction of the family.

In years gone by in Europe, and even today in many Asian countries, the family took responsibility for the function of social security. Having many children gave parents the security of knowing that they would be taken care of in their old age by their offspring. This familial form of self-responsibility should be appreciated and is very useful, because, as we know, the trend today in western countries is to shift responsibility onto the state, to the school, to the health care system, and other institutions outside the family, instead of taking care of our own problems in a responsible and self-conscious way.

3.2. Family life – a long and continuous process

3.2.1. The life-cycle approach in family life

Young people fall in love, marry, and have children. This is the beginning of a young family. Because of their attitude, lack of experience, and short-term challenges, young couples are focused on daily problems. For these reasons, discussions about long-term developments, i.e., the life-cycle course of the family and its members, can become a delicate matter. In spite of the difficulty discussing such issues, they are crucial for the future, and the family must be aware of this fact. Visions (and sometimes dreams) about the future will help the family to live a healthy and meaningful family life.

Investment in children (and parents) is worthwhile, and the return on investment is very high. Although life progresses and changes every day and every moment, principal decisions, such as those relating to education, association in the family, and exposure to the external environment, have a strong and long-lasting influence on family life.

Taking care of children is an ongoing task, regardless of the age of the children or the parents. If children grow up within a caring family, they will rely on their parents and ask for their support for as long as possible. Even if they sometimes don't admit it, they need assistance from their parents, especially in delicate situations, and they will come back and expect help from them.

Even with the disappearance of large families in recent years, grandparents are often asked by their children to help them with baby-sitting, gardening, teaching, taking care of pets, and other tasks. This is a win-win situation, because on the one hand, the younger generation can benefit from the skills and experience of the older generation, and on the other hand, grandparents are given meaningful tasks that can bring them fulfilment and satisfaction in their post-professional lives.

3.2.2. Conflict in the family

Living together in a limited space for many years naturally leads to many conflicts in family life. Conflicts between generations, but also disagreement between spouses, belong to daily life.
Because of our present social set up, it is fairly easy to "run away" from conflicts. Children can leave the family without difficulty at an early age and even divorce has become a relatively simple affair. Because of these new possibilities, family members are losing one of the greatest opportunities in family life, namely, open (and often painful) discussion and conflict-solving by compromise. Children who run away from home, couples who divorce because of minor disputes, feel the pinch afterwards. Children lose the real support of parents, divorcees lose the support of their spouses. In this way, new problems are

created that are much more severe than the conflicts that faced the family before. The wake-up call undoubtedly comes eventually, but in most cases it is too late.

Parents can help their children by teaching them at an early age to compromise and to give in when arguing about insignificant issues. In this way, much less friction is created within the family, and in the micro-environment around the family, positive energy is not wasted on unnecessary quarreling and can be used for other, useful tasks. The same applies to disputes between spouses. Conflicts between them can always be solved by conciliation, and a good idea is to think, when arguing, about the negative effects of a conflict that is unresolved.

Parents have to be united in front of their children because kids are smart enough to test the boundaries and will try time and again to cause conflict between parents. A good way of dealing with this challenge is to consult one's spouse before giving any binding answer to a child.

Another golden rule is not to carry family conflicts beyond the family. Many families have been broken because family members quarreled in front of "friends" or complete strangers, who interfered and gave "good" advice that led to much deeper conflict and even irreversible damage in the bond within the family. Such disputes have to be resolved within the family because family members know each other much better than strangers, and because outside interests do not have a place in such internal conflicts.

Parents have to be ready to compromise with their children. As mentioned above, disputes among generations are common, and usually the children, owing to their age and lack of experience, are unwilling to compromise. In such cases, parents have to decide how far they can go with concessions, but the basic will to embrace the opinions of their offspring must be there.

Finally, a golden rule is that persuasion is not selling our ideas or convincing opponents to see things our way. Effective persuasion is a process of learning and negotiating. This also applies to the unavoidable conflicts that occur in families.

3.3. The learning process in the family

Principally, most of the conclusions under 2.3., "Continuous learning," but especially those under 2.3.2., "A learning process," also apply to the learning process in the family.

Family support for children is extremely important in the educational procedure. Parents and grandparents, who are able to help children in primary and secondary school, enable them to enter high school without any problems worth mentioning. Parents and other family members with a higher education continue to support children in high school and even in college and university. Characteristically, it is not the most talented but the most intensively coached children go through high school, college, and university. Sadly enough, talented children who, for one reason or another, do not receive support from their family often abandon their studies at high school or university. Relatively few are able to complete their studies, but they are probably the best ones, because they have had to fight on their own, without any help, to graduate. These graduates usually have a steady and strong character, otherwise they wouldn't have been able to succeed.

Another phenomenon that has become more and more obvious in recent years is the knowledge gap between parents and children. Parents who do not invest in continuous learning may be caught off-guard by children, who grow up with globalization, the Internet, and personal computers. In those cases, children, even at a relatively early age, are much further along, regarding knowledge, behavior, and attitudes, than their parents are. Of course, the same can happen in schools with highly talented children and older teachers. To avoid, or at least to reduce, the problems resulting from this gap, parents (and teachers) have to seek to expose themselves to new technologies and to open discussion with the younger generation. A very important part of that discussion must be the subject of relativity regarding the new technologies and the importance of human relationships, especially these days, when many young people believe in the "absolute truth" of the results they get from computers, forgetting that computers cannot be smarter or cleverer than the developers who created the corresponding software.

Culture is a very important part in the learning process of the family. Music, theater, literature, and exposure to other cultures are often neglected in the environment outside the family. Variety also means change, but constant exposure to cultural affairs means continuity. The importance of culture in the family, including all the generations, cannot be stressed enough. This early exposure will often be the trigger for creativity, excellent human relations, and other extraordinary achievements in later years.

3.4. <u>Social competence in family life</u>

Parents are responsible for taking care of the social features of the family. These aspects can be divided into internal and external facets. The internal part includes equal treatment of all members of the family, hospitality, and the nurturing of friends of the family, especially those of the children. The external part will be treated later separately.

Equal treatment of grandparents and all children helps to prevent conflict and hard feelings in the family. Even if parents are fond of one child more than they are of another, children should not feel any discrimination. In addition, if grandparents are old and cannot be of much help anymore, they have to be treated in a honorable manner. They were the ones who originally created the family.

Hospitality gives a lot of satisfaction. Through it, the family unit comes into contact with many external individuals who can contribute to the family's experience of diversity and the fostering of tolerance toward others. Moreover, by hosting the friends of the children, it is much easier for the parents to defuse potentially negative influences on them by monitoring for smoking, drug use, alcohol abuse, etc. Acquaintance with the children's friends also helps parents to understand the way of thinking of the own children much better.

Social competence, if exercised correctly and continuously, generates a good feeling among all family members. They know that under difficult conditions, they can count on each other and that they will receive help from the family. They know that in their family, everybody helps everybody.

Part Four: Social Lifetime

4.1. Continuity in social life

Although we live in a modern and progressive world, there are still three basic political systems: democracy, oligarchy, and dictatorship. The following reflections are related to democratic systems, which are characteristic of most of today's western countries.

Society is usually more inert than families and businesses are, so the principle of continuity in public life is even more important than it is in the private or corporate sphere. Even small achievements in social life are products of long years of effort and the will to compromise. Being social creatures, human beings cannot survive without interacting with society in all aspects, so we all need to understand that, particularly with regard to the public sphere, things move slowly and not always in the direction we would like to see.

From time to time, we witness "leaps" in social life, such as the opening of a new theater or changes in political systems. In such cases, we get the feeling of a "sudden" change. Looking behind the scenes, however, we can see that all those changes are the result of long and continuous processes. Insiders know that relentless efforts over a long period preceded the "abrupt" change.

4.1.1. The value of continuity in social life

Continuity prevails in history, whether for good or bad.

Political systems, such as democracy, are the result of processes that have gone on for centuries. Naturally, the question arises, "Why do we actually need whole centuries to establish such a system, which most of us are happy with, and which replaced previous forms of rule and government in which human rights were not a real issue?" The answer is a very complex and subtle one and lies within the very same complexity of life and society. Behind every system, there are powerful groups that try, because of their particular interests, to maintain the status quo at all costs. Furthermore, as already mentioned before, most human beings do not like change and therefore are opposed to new systems and processes. However, the basic demand for better and more righteous systems was so strong that, despite this resistance, change took gradually place. This change would not have occurred without continuity and resolution.

We can also find continuity on the "negative" side of history. If we look back at social issues like racial discrimination, religious wars, and ethnic conflicts, it is clear that they are also processes that go on for centuries, or even longer. Again, powerful interest groups stand behind these evils. There is no other way to fight such wickedness except through continuous processes, such as education, personal persuasion, and the like. Perseverance is here the name of the game, too, and the struggle against them will bear fruit only if it is as determined and uncompromising as the attitude on the other side, which caused the injustice and pain.

From the above, it is possible to see that, in social life, too, continuity and persistence are the common denominators that constitute the difference between success and failure.

4.1.2. Perseverance in social life

In democratic countries, social and political decisions are the result of lengthy and time-consuming processes. They usually represent compromises between different opinions and attitudes.

This means that in order to effect change in such systems, the individuals involved have to be persistent and patient.

4.1.3. Flexibility in social life

When dealing with inert and powerful systems, authorities, and officials, individuals are challenged to show a great deal of flexibility. Bureaucracy is not famous for being especially flexible. Officials are usually experts in their own specific field, while ordinary citizens who deal with particular issues in those fields are limited in the time they have to learn all the aspects of a particular subject. On the other hand, common people can come up with unusual but sound suggestions for improvements that are not considered by the officials dealing with the issues. The result of such situations, time and again, is that small changes are implemented in existing systems and processes; it often occurs slowly and little by little, but even this is preferable to the alternative of keeping things as they were, if things were unsatisfactory.

Daily contact with fellow citizens also demands a lot of flexibility. As mentioned before, our society is composed of numerous interest groups, and it is only natural that in every day life one group will try to impose its ideas on others. By being flexible, we can reach acceptable compromises in these cases, too (more on this subject will follow under 4.2.2).

4.1.4. Short- and long-term aspects of social life

As in all other facets of life, rewards for efforts relating to social life can realistically be expected only in the long run. Nevertheless, our efforts have to go on, day by day, if we are to achieve our goals.

Slow (and not-so-slow) changes can take place in western societies because of large-scale immigration from remote countries with different cultures. The phenomenon is not new; only the scale is without precedent. The "natives" of western countries are faced with the major challenge of opening themselves to alien cultures and habits and of creating a symbiosis between those and their own cultures. Even children in primary schools are confronted with foreign languages and habits. Successful integration is depends very much on the attitude of those children and the support they get from their parents in this respect.

Children are more flexible and adaptive than adults are. Consequently, clashes between cultures occur much more often between adults than among children. It is sometimes difficult to see the long-term reward of giving up part of our own cultural tradition, but actually this is an evolutionary process that was already ongoing in former days, even if at a slower pace. The trend in the west is to become international and global, so national states will gradually disappear in the not-too-distant future. By exhibiting modesty and bringing our own desires for individuality under control will help in this melting-pot process. Moreover, the increased globalization in the variety of consumer goods and the increasing range of adventures on offer will help to bridge the gap between different cultures. Behaving appropriately in the short term will help this evolutionary process in the long run.

We are living today in a society with a great variety of options, but alongside this there runs a growing demand for orientation, knowledge, and opinion with regard to all processes. Especially after numerous horrendous and violent events in the United States and other western countries, second thoughts are expressed about the "fun society." A return to basic social values, such as humanity, solidarity, and truly equal rights to all, can be foreseen.

4.2. Social life – an extended and permanent process

In this era of globalization, the influence of a single person on society is double-edged. On the one hand, systems and processes are getting so huge and complex that the individual even has problems understanding "what is going on" around him/her. On the other hand, the very same complex systems, i.e., the Internet, empower us, as individuals, to change things in our surroundings. We just have to fight for our ideas with perseverance and determination. Furthermore, we have to start small, in our own micro-environment, where we are familiar with the critical issues and can find alliances.

The generation that grew up after the Second World War witnessed the creation of political entities like the Eastern and Western Blocs but also saw the establishment of a universal political institution: the United Nations. The next generation already saw this situation as a fact of life and was stirred into life by the disruption of the Eastern Bloc at the end of the 1980s. At that time, only one superpower was left on our planet and economic forces gradually became the strongest element in our environment. The era of a neo-liberalism started, and politics became more and more a mouthpiece for those economic forces. Then 9/11 happened, and once again politics became the leading element in life. However, after this shock was digested, politics once again became increasingly influenced by commerce.

These changes demanded a great deal from individuals. We were used to fighting for our ideals for many years only to discover later that many of those principles were not so glamorous or even all that relevant anymore. Then the fight against the overwhelming power of economics became a major challenge in the life of many individuals. We were not so sure any more that the capitalist system was superior to the socialist one. As soon as the socialist system had been considerably weakened, capitalism took over and ruled according to its own interests, resulting in increasing wealth but also increasing poverty, along with a rise in the number of jobless people and growing social unrest in many places.

The main challenge for all of us in this demanding process is not to lose sight of our goals and to stick to our individual principles, even during difficult times. The principles of helping the disadvantaged members of society remained present and tangible during all those years, and only if every one of us participates in this important social process in our own micro-environment will mankind be able to defuse serious conflict and avoid the kinds of wars and destruction like those we see in more than fifty countries around the world today.

4.2.1. The life-cycle approach in social life

A family is exposed to society in many ways and is dependent on the social order.

Children go through the educational systems: primary, secondary and high schools, colleges and universities. In all those years, they are part of the school class, which can be either a wonderful team or just a bunch of individuals, depending on the spirit that prevails in the class. If parents produce team players, their children will become leaders or an important part of the team in school. This attribute will accompany them during their whole lifetime, bringing them success and satisfaction over many years.

When basic education is completed and children become adults, they will be exposed to the workplace, but also to social life. If they can make friends and create alliances with people in the outside world, they will be able to influence processes going on at both micro and macro levels, avoiding unpleasant surprises, such as nasty changes in their immediate surroundings. Good opportunities can be found for young adults through membership of political parties or professional societies. Continuous and diligent work in such circles is rewarding in the long run and stays with such "social workers" through to old age. Voluntary work in professional societies or other social institutions offers variety and opportunities but also valuable connections to people outside the individual's personal micro-environment. Such connections can be very helpful from various points of view.

Voluntary work for the public is usually an additional task on top of other activities. Moreover, there is little financial incentive to carry out public work. Consequently, it is not easy to find people who are willing to do voluntary work. However, because of the ever-increasing number of elderly citizens, voluntary work in communities, societies, and institutions becomes an interesting option to use available time in a meaningful way. Elderly people also have the opportunity to participate in social life. In this way, they are not excluded from society but are regarded as useful members of the community. Opportunities are there to help the disadvantaged, to teach children, to work in community centers, and more besides. Such activities give fulfilment to the lives of the elderly. They avoid feeling that their life is already finished or that they are useless. Seniors can look back on long years' experience in many fields, and while performing social tasks, they can take full advantage of their knowledge. By tackling new opportunities, their social competence grows and from time to time we can see the spectacular achievements of senior citizens in the fields of public health, education, and community service, among others.

4.2.2. Conflicts within society

As indicated under 4.1.3., conflicts exist in society because of the existence of many interest groups and divergent ideas about the solutions to many problems and challenges in our society.

As a relevant example, one can consider the ever-growing number of laws and rules in all countries of the world. Millions of lawyers are occupied with the creation of new laws, aiming to cover more and more cases with regard to the possible violation of existing legislation. Needless to say, the more laws that are generated, the more loopholes and the more contradictions between different laws and rules exist.

Recent occurrences with regard to the activities of intelligence agencies caused a vigorous discussion about the personal freedom of citizens in western countries. On the one hand, most of us understand that everything has to be done to curb terrorism, because this phenomenon is a threat to our very existence. On the other hand, excessive restraint on our personal freedom is not acceptable because we live in a democratic culture in which citizens have to possess certain rights, especially those connected to personal freedom. The name of the game here is to find the right balance between fighting terrorism and the restrictions on personal freedom. This is a great challenge to politicians, but also to all members of society.

Because of the very existence of democracy, conflicts between countries can turn into conflicts between citizens. Often, this happens because the official politics of a particular country are not supported by the people. On the one hand, political processes have become very complex, while on the other hand, huge blocs, like the European Union, NAFTA, and other trade organizations, have been created in recent decades.

A good example of such a dispute is the introduction of a common currency in the member countries of the European Union. A number of member countries did not want to join this currency because of the resistance of their citizens, who were proud of and wanted to keep their national currency. In other countries, there was considerable resistance against the introduction because people feared about losing the strength and buying power of their national currencies. The nearer the date of introduction came, the less resistance was registered in those countries, mainly as a result of the intensive explanatory work by officials, banks, and other relevant institutions. Even so, resistance still exists, and we can only hope that it will decrease with the wider acceptance of the euro.

Discussion about environmental protection in recent years is another relevant case. On one side of the fence, the United States, Australia, and China were reluctant to sign the Kyoto protocol, while on the other side were several European countries that are leaders in the handling of environmental issues. In the west, there are also internal conflicts between, on the one hand, Greenpeace and other environmental organizations and, on the other hand, governments and economic forces. However, climate change is a fact of life now, and frequent natural catastrophes are going to force all nations to take the necessary measures to prevent disasters or minimize their impact.

Growing poverty in western countries is also a source of social conflict. A growing world population and vast differences in the standard of living between and within countries cause ongoing turbulence all over the world. The same poverty is also a fertile soil for violence, civil wars, and aggression in general. In virtually every country on our planet, TV channels like CNN, Sky News, and others are readily available. Poor people in third-world countries watch those stations and become fascinated by the wealth of the western world. This provides further cause for conflict, and a solution within the near future is not foreseeable. However, this cannot be an excuse for refraining from dealing with the problem with determination. Only if every single member of human society is aware of this crisis and fights it actively will it be overcome. Individuals can pinpoint problems and challenges in their micro-environment and help needy persons directly and efficiently. In this way, everyone can be sure to have taken at least a tiny step in the right direction. By a common effort, each person has a chance to defuse this severe conflict. The conflicts have to be resolved with the highest priority, because the alternative is destruction and annihilation.

Another example is personal conflict with other members of society within our own environment. This can happen because of diverging interests regarding communal affairs, clashes with neighbors on property issues or noise, educational and behavior issues of children, and more. In these conflicts, there is no space for pride or stubbornness. Even as individuals, we have to keep our eyes on the common interests of society. By resolving social trouble, we also solve our own problems. If we insult some of our fellow citizens, we should not be too proud to apologize. In particular, in such cases we have a chance to make friends instead of making enemies.

4.3. The learning process in society

As at home and in the workplace, integration in society means continuous learning and exposure to social processes, both traditional and new.

The education system is going through a transformative phase, and the result will be new kinds of schools that teach the scholar, above all, how to learn. Thanks to the Internet and other digital databases, any necessary information is immediately available to students. The problem is how to make use of the huge quantity of accessible information. How is it possible to find out which bit of the available information is needed? What is the most efficient procedure to reach the required piece of information as fast as possible?

Schools at all levels have to cope with financial restrictions; their means are limited, and they understand that specific learning at a higher level and related to particular subjects, is carried out today by corporations and institutions, which are in need of specific know-how. Consequently, in addition to the issues mentioned above, schools have been left with two important areas to deal with:

- Basic studies.
- Highly innovative and creative projects that are ahead of the industry.

Being public institutions, schools were not exposed in the past to severe competition. Because of financial restrictions, this is changing now, and private schools are competing fiercely with public institutions. As a result, public schools are being forced to undergo changes, too, and the process is going on with full power just now.

As indicated under 2.3, continuous learning is a necessity everywhere. People dealing professionally or voluntarily with public tasks have to take care of their ongoing education, too. Basically, the guidelines mentioned under 2.3 also apply in the public sector. The pressure on intensive and fast learning may be somewhat higher in industry, but the learning process is part of life in all sectors. Society expects people at all levels to learn continuously. This demand is a new challenge to all of us and causes social problems because some parts of society were not required to take part in this process of continuous learning in the past.

4.4. Competence in social life

In order to be accepted by society, individuals have to demonstrate social competence. Some examples of this are:

- Philanthropy and charity.
- Aid for third-world countries.
- Harmony in human relationships.
- Taking responsibility for oneself.
- Friendliness towards fellow citizens.
- Public work.

Various people have become very rich in recent years. Many of them are still young and originated in the middle class. Their wealth comes mainly from the recent development of the e-society. Although many of them have recently lost some of their wealth, it is still so great that it impossible for them to use their assets only for themselves. Because of their background and career, many of them look to invest part of their wealth in meaningful projects, among them ventures that would promote the activities of very young people with start-ups or projects in third-world countries. With regard to pure charity, poverty old and new pose an important challenge to western societies, and there is a place for charity in our world. New ways of distributing funds have to be found, however, because in many places charity does not reach the needy, it is ending up instead in the pockets of corrupt and unscrupulous "leaders" in the targeted countries. More and more often, it is possible to see examples of direct aid sent to third-world countries, in which assets are sent by aid organizations directly to projects that are identified as worthy of support.

Respecting other people in society is a rewarding attitude that also gives us self-respect. Unfortunately, it is not an attitude found everywhere. This should not be an excuse not to treat other people correctly, however. Paying respect to others soon becomes mutual, and in this way we witness a revaluation of our own personality.

The existing social structures in western countries fool many of us into surrendering responsibility to institutions outside the family. Some examples are children's educational problems, which we expect schools and teachers to solve, and problems in the workplace, which might lead us to leave a job and expect the state to provide for our own shortcomings in form of social support. This attitude is quite dangerous because by giving up self-responsibility, we lose control over our own lives. We are less and less able to master life and create serious problems in our personal sphere. It is for this very reason that it is crucial for all of us to take responsibility for ourselves, to deal with our own problems, and to find solutions, be it in the family or another private sphere. In the short term, this is difficult, but in the long run this approach pays off because it helps us to avoid much graver problems in the future.

Smiling, or approaching our fellow citizens in a friendly way, can create wonders. In big cities, in big corporations, or in big public places, the feeling of being alone is a very real one. Taking the initiative and approaching other people with a small question or remark or by starting a small conversation brings joy to other people, but also to us. More than once, valuable personal relations have started through such a small step. The reward is great and immediate.

Epilogue

For various reasons, this essay has lain on my desk for ten years. Because of other priorities, I did not find the time to review and finish it.

Amazingly enough, reviewing the whole work, I found that I had only to replace or correct a few passages and sentences. This was the best proof for me that continuity, in spite of the many "changes" I had experienced in those ten years, prevails.

Unfortunately, the last ten years have been marked by many conflicts, often resulting in regional wars and international tension, as well as the financial crisis that started in 2008 and which is not yet solved. This fact influences various aspects of our life.

In those ten years I was also engaged in activities dealing with the history of mankind. This subject is particularly interesting because it deals with continuity, even though changes have accompanied mankind through its thousands of years. The more I studied history, the more I came to the conclusion that "nothing is new under the sun." Even if we look at high technology, the basis for today's achievements were already in development a long time ago, and that development was itself a continuous process.

Altogether, I am even more convinced than I was ten years ago that our present way of life is the result of countless small steps and the hard work of former generations. I very much hope that this modest work will help to convince the reader to take a "helicopter view" of life, dealing with the different aspects as a whole. If I succeed in achieving that goal, all the effort was worth the trouble.

Ebmatingen, Switzerland, February 2015.

1st Edition, February 2015

© Copyright Mobifit GmbH, Ebmatingen, Switzerland

Notes:

Herstellung und Verlag:
BoD - Books on Demand, Norderstedt
ISBN 978-3-7347-8557-3